SEVERANCE/

D SET/DISCIP

ER/COURAGE

CE/FIGHTERS

CIPLINE/WILL

GE/PERSEVER

RS MIND SET

WILLPOWER/

RSEVERANCE/

D SET/5 KEYS

FIGHTER

FIVE KEYS **TO CONQUERING FEAR AND REACHING YOUR DREAMS**

MANAFEST

CHRISTOPHER GREENWOOD SHANNON CONSTANTINE LOGAN

Manafest
PRODUCTIONS
Inc.

DEDICATION

Dedicated to my beautiful wife and best friend Melanie.
You have stood by my side and taught me never to give up!
If it weren't for your constant support, love and encouragement
I wouldn't be the man I am today.
You have watched me perform, speak and rock crowds of
thousands. You are also there to catch me when I collapse into bed
at night. You see me at my best and my worst and love me just the
same. You truly know what it means to be a Fighter,
I love you!

FIGHTER

FIVE KEYS TO CONQUERING FEAR
AND REACHING YOUR DREAMS

NEVER QUIT!
PROVERBS 24:16

For information about special discounts for bulk purchases, please contact Manafest Productions for special sales at: info@imafighter.net

Author: Christopher Greenwood *A.K.A. MANAFEST*

Written by: Christopher Greenwood & Shannon Constantine Logan

Edited by: Carissa Bluestone & Shannon Constantine Logan

Art Direction & Design by: Melanie Greenwood *WWW.VISIONCITY.BIZ*

Contributing Photography by: Melanie Greenwood & Chris Stacey

Manufactured in China

ISBN: 978-0-9891603-0-8

WWW.MANAFEST.NET
WWW.IMAFIGHTER.NET

NO PLAN B

IT'S TOO LATE
IT'S MY FATE
I CAN'T TURN AROUND

THERE'S NO FEAR
IN THE MIRROR
TO HOLD ME DOWN

I'M TOO FAR
FROM THE START
NOW I'M IN TOO DEEP

I'VE GOT TO STICK TO THE PLAN
CAUSE THERE IS NO PLAN B

NO TURNING BACK
THERE'S NO OTHER PATH

AND I KNOW
THAT THIS ROAD
IS MY DESTINY

I'VE GOT TO STICK TO THE PLAN
CAUSE THERE IS NO PLAN B

-MANAFEST
LYRICS FROM THE SONG "NO PLAN B", *THE CHASE* ALBUM

INTRO // **A FATHER IS LOST, A FIGHTER IS BORN** *1*
"It's not about how you start, but how you finish"
—Manafest

CHAPTER ONE // **COURAGE** *20*
"The greatest battles of life are fought out daily in the
silent chambers of the soul." —David O. McKay

CHAPTER TWO // **PERSEVERANCE** *40*
"We must be willing to let go of the life we planned so as
to have the life that is waiting for us." —Joseph Campbell

CHAPTER THREE // **FIGHTER'S MIND SET** *64*
"You can chain me, you can torture me, you can even
destroy this body, but you will never imprison my mind."
—Mahatma Gandhi

CHAPTER FOUR // **DISCIPLINE** *84*
"The first and best victory is to conquer self." —Plato

CHAPTER FIVE // **WILLPOWER** *108*
"Life doesn't hand you your dreams." —Dave Ramsey

CHAPTER SIX // **KNOCK OUT** *127*
"I was born a male, but chose to be a man. When I became
a man, I also became a fighter, and when I became a
fighter, I started walking in my destiny." —Manafest

CHAPTER SEVEN // **DREAMS, VISIONS & GOALS** *139*
"The best way to predict your future is to create it."
—Abraham Lincoln

A FATHER IS LOST A FIGHTER IS BORN

I was born on July 19, 1979 at Centenary Hospital in Scarborough, Ontario, Canada. I grew up in a small city outside of Toronto called Pickering, an underdeveloped area with lots of farmland. My mother's parents emigrated from England, arriving in Quebec City on May 2, 1931 on the White Star Line. My mother said the name of the ship was the Laurentic, a British ocean liner that served the Liverpool–Quebec City route in the early 1900s. I'm an English boy, the youngest in my family, with one sister, Virginia, who is four years older than me. We lived on a street called Malden Crescent in a four-bedroom house with a balcony attached, so you could walk out at night and look at the stars. I played in those big dirty hills around my house, surrounded by the bleached skeletons of framed houses going up, and construction crews all around, digging holes and drilling.

I watched the city transform. I remember finding a lot of new streets when I was a kid.

There was a lot of anger and resentment in our house, but despite that, my childhood wasn't abnormal. We were spoiled rotten, and my sister and I fought like cats and dogs, but we had some good moments, too. I remember peaceful nights of just sitting on the balcony with my mom, gazing at the stars and wishing for things. I remember riding my bike around the streets, playing hide-and-seek with my friends for fun, and walking home from school with icicles growing from my nose, in snowstorms so thick you could barely see the trees in front of you. I'd push open my front door to be greeted by a steaming bowl of tomato soup, a plate of macaroni and cheese, and an episode of Spider-Man. I was a typical young boy—on a Saturday morning you would find me cuddled up on the couch with my favorite blanket and a bowl of Froot Loops in my lap, watching cartoons.

The only problem was that I didn't know God's love back then; there was too much darkness.

"Does it really do much good to light one tiny candle in all this darkness? Yes, there is always hope."
—"Og" Mandino

THE DARK CLOUD

It was a spring afternoon when a dark cloud descended on my house, and brought ambulances, fire trucks, and police cars blazing up my street. I was too young to understand what was going on and I can barely remember what happened, because my mother did such a good job of shielding me. My sister led me to McDonald's while the police were at the house, to shelter me from the storm.

I don't know how I found out. Maybe it was my mom…I don't

know. But someone must have sat me down to explain why my dad was gone and would never return. When you're five years old, I'm not sure if I would have understood what suicide was anyway.

That day my dad drank and took some pills and went down to the basement and hung himself. He was thirty-eight. My mother discovered his body hanging there and raced up the stairs, beating the steps with her clenched fists asking God, "Why?" This was his third suicide attempt, and it was successful. My mom told me she had caught him once trying to slit his wrists, and he'd promised her he'd never go through with it. I've never asked further about their conversations. I do know that shortly before he died, my dad was admitted to the psychiatric ward of a local hospital. He was there three weeks when the doctors let him leave for the weekend. He was supposed to return to the hospital that night, but he never did. Thinking about it now, it still doesn't make sense. He'd just gotten released after being in the hospital for attempting suicide. You'd think his friends and family would have been around to support him. But then again, maybe everything was kept secret out of shame. I don't know.

My father was a workaholic so I don't have many memories of him. I know he had a job in downtown Toronto at a stock brokerage firm, but it wasn't until I was older that I found out he suffered from depression, anxiety, and low self-esteem. My mother told me my father had a difficult childhood; his dad was a heavy drinker and always picked on him, and made him feel like he wasn't good enough. I'm sure that's where his low self-image stemmed from. One of my earliest memories of my grandfather was when I was around 4 years old. Before my dad passed away, I remember he took me somewhere with his father. We were standing in a parking lot, and my grandfather started cussing at me, dropping a lot of f-bombs.

I was so hurt and angry; I wished my dad had stuck up for me.

It must have made an impression because it's one of the few days with my dad that I can remember. Our time together never lasted long, as I think he struggled in relating to his children. I remember only one Christmas with my father, and him playing G.I. Joes with me. I know I must have begged him to play with me constantly, but the times when he did were few and far between; otherwise I'd have more memories.

There were times in my life as a teenager when I wondered what life would be like if he were still alive. Would I still be singing? Would I have been more confident because I had a father in my life? Or would things have been jacked up anyway? Today, as a grown man, when I think about his death, it bothers me even more, because I can't imagine ever neglecting my kids. I still wonder what type of demons haunt people's minds and push them to take their own lives. How hard can life be? What kind of guy kills himself when he has a wife and two children?

I believe the day of the funeral was the first time I realized my dad wasn't coming home. It was an open casket ceremony for family only, and my cousin dared me to touch one of his eyes. My mother must have thought I was just going up to look at him one last time as I crept towards the casket, but when my hand reached out toward his face, all hell broke loose. I was such a little punk. I don't know if I was numb or just too young to understand, but I don't remember shedding a tear. I can still see my family that day crying, and everyone was upset but me. My father must have had very little involvement in my life, because when he was gone there was nothing to miss. How could I miss someone I didn't even know?

We sold the house my dad died in a little more than a year later; my mother didn't want to be reminded of my father every time she walked downstairs to do laundry. We leased an apartment for a few months while waiting for our new house to be built. This put a lot of stress on my mom because the builder never met deadlines. (The interesting thing is that when my mom went to sign the lease on the apartment, the lady she dealt with at the rental office happened to be the mother of Melanie, the girl I'd marry seventeen years later. Coincidence? I think not.)

My mother is a strong woman and has always loved, prayed for, and provided for my older sister and me. She really went out of her way to make sure we were OK and constantly looked after us. My mother and I have always shared a close bond, and even when I was in the wrong, she always supported and loved me. I cried many tears growing up, and she was there to comfort me. I know she put her children before herself, which I will always be grateful for. She is one of my many great examples of what a fighter is. After the loss of my dad, she put her faith in God and found the strength that got us through those dark times.

I get my strength from my mom, so even back then I was a fighter, but it was the wrong kind of fighting.

At school I was starting to quickly become a class clown and a bully; I'd push kids down on the playground during recess and get into it with other students. In second grade I remember throwing my pencil up in the air, and making noises and jokes while our teacher was trying to read to us. I got sent to the principal's office more than once and was given my own private desk in the corner of the classroom. But the bullying and clowning didn't stop. Eventually they separated me from the class to what was called an "opportunity class" with a different teacher. I had to attend this class every afternoon until my grades improved and I got my act together.

Even among these students I felt like an outcast; these kids were much more mischievous than me, so I worked my butt off to get out of there. Now my mom laughs at all the times she would get calls from the principal's office telling her that I'd set off fireworks or gotten into another fistfight. One time, on the way home from school, I got into a fight with a kid who smacked me in the face with the end of his backpack and gave me a bloody nose. He ran away and I tried to chase him down the sidewalk, but I was too chubby to catch him. What a punk.

For fifth and sixth grades I attended William Dunbar Public School, and I was constantly in trouble. To deal with my problems, I turned to food for comfort. I loved donuts, pizza, barbecue potato chips, and cream soda. My mom took me out to eat all the time—getting me cheeseburgers, fries, and yes, donuts. During pizza day at school, I would always get two pizzas instead of one. Food became a crutch I leaned on to deal with my issues at school. I was a pale, freckle-faced kid and I weighed almost 120 pounds. Considering that I was barely over five feet tall, that's a lot of weight for a kid my age! This made me insecure, shy, and less confident in everything I did, and the students were always making fun of me for my weight or the clothes I wore. (To be honest, I had no fashion style at all until like grade eight, so maybe I was asking for it.) The school playground can be a cruel and intimidating place for kids, and it sure was for me. I'd get bullied, picked on, and I'd hang out with friends who were so insecure that depending on who was around, some days they'd be my friends, and other days they'd turn on me. I got a lot of that when I was younger.

One particular kid comes to mind; his name was Ryan. My mother had a day job while I was in fifth and sixth grade, and for three months, she dropped me off at Ryan's house before school.

His mom ran a daycare and they'd look after me until I got picked up after school. I wasn't very popular in public school, and Ryan wasn't cool either. Physically my opposite, he was a tall, lanky white kid who played a lot of video games—a borderline geek. And for a long time he wouldn't hang out with me. We would walk to school together every day, but when we'd get within a few yards of the building, he'd dart ahead of me because he didn't want to be seen with me. That hurt. It really ticked me off, too. Our friendship continued to run hot and cold like that for years, and mostly I just accepted it. But one day, when we were in high school, we were hanging out in front of a friend's house, goofing off, making fun of each other and I don't remember what he said, but I was just waiting for any reason to snap. I got him in a headlock, threw him to the ground, and left him there. I laughed, stuck my middle finger up at him and pressed it against the window, as I drove off. Not a proud moment in my life, but it was inevitable. After hearing all the hurtful comments thrown at me in school like, "Greenwood, you're a loser!" and "You're not a leader, you're a follower!" I eventually found other kids I could lash out at so I'd feel better about myself. You really do become a product of your environment.

By high school I was a totally different person. I took my classes seriously, I had friends, and I lost a lot of weight. Even as skinny as I am today, I'm still very conscious of my weight, because I never want to be fat again. I would dream about being skinny. I hated my big stomach so much that in the shower I'd grab my gut and I would punch it saying, "I hate you." When I did finally start to lose weight, I starved myself—eating less than normal, but still trying to exercise more. I'd drink those Slim-Fast shakes that were heavily advertised on TV. Every morning instead of a big bowl of Froot Loops, it was a Slim-Fast shake. I don't recommend starving yourself, but I do encourage not eating junk food and exercising regularly. It literally felt like one day I was fat, and the next day I was skinny. I didn't notice I had lost so much weight until people started making comments. One day a girl said to me, "Greenwood, you're wearing jeans. I've never seen you wear jeans." I said to her, "That's because I could never fit into a pair that looked good on me."

Ephesians 2:10 — "For we are God's masterpiece. He has created us anew in Christ Jesus, so we can do the good things he planned for us long ago."

God still had a plan for my life, even if my mom had to drag me to church kicking and screaming. Every Sunday morning, fifteen minutes before it was time to go, I would creep silently into a closet and hide. I could hear her yelling, "Christopher Scott, get down here now, or you're grounded!" But I wouldn't say a word. Eventually, she would give up and leave me there. After I heard the door slam, I would run to the side window and peek through the blinds to watch the car pull away. Once she turned the corner, I would feel guilty and think, I should have gone with her.

When I did go to church, it was uncomfortable. Some of the people were nice, but some of them were just plain weirdos. There were a few people I liked, though, like the six-foot-tall white man with the bright-white beard and a smile that stretched across the room. He intrigued me. The second his foot hit the platform he had the whole church standing, singing, and clapping to the beat. I always enjoyed singing the songs when he was leading because he made me smile, even if I was angry about being there. I remember the old-school hymnals smelled funny, like the pews they'd been sitting in for so many years. Singing at church could be considered my early beginnings in music, even though I didn't know it at the time.

When it came time for the pastor to preach, I wanted to run out of there. And sometimes I did! I would pretend I had to go to the bathroom and get up to pass the time elsewhere because it was so boring. Eventually, I'd go back in or just sit in the car and wait for my mom and sister. I couldn't connect to God on that level; I had nothing to relate to. I strongly believe if there had been better youth programs at that time, I would have understood faith, love, and respect on a child's level. I'd be even stronger today. But I'm not feeling bitter, just making a point about the times I grew up in. Nowadays there are many great youth programs for kids to plug into.

Luckily, God had other means to deliver the same messages to me that I couldn't have gotten from my experiences at church.

GOD SENDS AN ANGEL

Not long after my father's death, God sent a young man into my life by the name of Bruce. He must have heard about my father's death because he approached my mother one day in church, offering to be my friend. He was nineteen at the time, and he must have been concerned that I didn't have an older male figure in my life. He wanted to be that example for me.

Bruce began to hang out with me regularly, taking me on hikes, playing board games with me, and bringing me with him to youth church on Wednesdays. He was right: I looked up to him like a father, and clung to him immediately. Bruce taught me what it meant to give. He was a young man when he started investing his time in me. He could have been out chasing girls or hanging out with his friends, but instead, he poured thousands of hours into my life. I'm eternally grateful for that. As time went on and we grew closer, I helped him clean the church, and fix small things, like computers. Bruce was a teacher at the Durham Business & Computer College, and taught me how to back up the school's computer systems. My favorite part was taking a break to eat barbecue potato chips and drink sodas. One night, while stuffing my face with chips and changing floppy disks, he sat me down in his office and shared the story of Jesus with me. I was seven years old. I didn't fully understand what it all meant, but I knew enough that I was sure I didn't want to go to hell. So, that night, with Bruce guiding me, I invited Jesus into my life as my Lord and Savior.

I believe this was a huge turning point in a spiritual sense. Not that I didn't have problems in middle school and high school, but I believe I would have had even more struggles if I hadn't had God and his angels looking out for me from that moment on. I gave permission for God to turn my life around, and put myself in position to be blessed. It was like a curse was removed from the Greenwood family; there would be generations to come that would serve and honor God.

I couldn't have asked for a better role model in my life than Bruce. He introduced me to Jesus and taught me the Bible, and the computer skills paid off, too, because later that became one of my first day jobs. I built my first computer at twelve years old and eventually attended the college Bruce owned called Durham Business & Computer College in Scarborough, Ontario. Bruce and I are still great friends. He stood by my side as best man at my wedding and continues to support me in everything I do. He's been at almost every music video shoot and at many of my concerts and is always ready to lend a helping hand.

The reason I share my story is to not glorify the past, but give hope for the future. If God can rescue me and turn my life around, he can do the same for you. The truth is, life sucks sometimes, but God truly is "the Father to the fatherless" (Psalms 68:5).

ANATOMY OF A FIGHTER

I never wanted to be a musician. Picture a shy white kid with baggy jeans, blonde hair, scabs on his elbows, and a skateboard: I was the epitome of Canadian suburbia. It was 1993, I was fourteen years old, and Eminem had just barely broken onto the scene. The only white rappers I could relate to were the Beastie Boys, but only because they had skateboarding in their videos. I never lay awake dreaming about stages, music videos, or traveling the world. I had one dream: to be a professional skateboarder living in California, doing demos, and filming skate videos. I wanted to have my own skateboard with my name on it and my own customized shoe design. If someone told me that in four years I would learn how to rap, and that one day I would be speaking and performing in front of thousands of people, I'd have laughed in their face. You might as well have told me I'd be a UFC fighter or a lion tamer, because that's how ridiculous it would have sounded.

I started skating when I was fourteen years old, and stopped when I was 18; my skateboarding career ended abruptly and life took a new direction. I fell in love with music. When I was twenty, I joined a group, rocked the open mics in downtown Toronto, and started booking shows. Fast Forward and I was twenty-five years old and $30,000 in debt, traveling around North America, living what I thought was going to be a rap star's dream. I hadn't seen my wife in over three weeks, no one was coming to my shows, and no one was buying my music. Push fast forward again, I'm 27 years old... It's 2007 and I'd just released the album Glory. It blew up in Japan, selling 40,000 records and over 80,000 singles, which breathed new life into my career. I signed with EMI Japan, recorded the album The Chase, which became a global hit; I received music grants and was nominated for two JUNO awards. Today, I've toured in twelve different countries, sold over 200,000 records worldwide, and had songs on the top ten billboard charts, major sport networks, TV shows, and featured in video games—and I've watched my songs become anthems for thousands of people all over the world.

How did I make this happen? I had to change my attitude to change my life.

WHY MANAFEST?

A lot of people ask me where I got the name Manafest. When I decided to go solo, I needed a stage name. I wanted to be called "Speedy," because that was my nickname in high school, but none of my hip-hop friends liked it. The idea of Manafest came to me while I was on the phone with a friend of mine, but instead of spelling it with an i spell it with an a. At the time, it didn't have any meaning to me at all except that it sounded cool. I wanted my music style to define me more then my name did. It's all about the music anyway. Then I started to think about it. When something is made manifest, it's because the light has exposed it. I've always wanted my music and my life to be a light to encourage people, whether I'm writing, or performing, or speaking in front of a crowd.

Last year I realized that I was reaching people with my message, but there wasn't enough time to go in-depth with what's in my heart and mind. In a song, I have only three or four minutes to tell a story or share my viewpoint. And even offstage I only get five or ten minutes with most people, one on one. The more I thought about it, the more I dreamed of what it would be like to write a book. How many people could I inspire beyond my music? How many books have I been inspired by? What if I didn't write it?

Writing a book was scary; it was completely outside my comfort zone of music and the safety of the great production team I work with, but I didn't let the fear of the unknown stop me. I began noting my ideas on my smartphone as I traveled. I'd jot down my thoughts wherever I was: on the plane, driving in the van, or hanging out with friends. Before I knew it I had amassed a ton of ideas, outlines, and a solid draft of the first few thousand words. My excitement grew. One day I was flying home from a tour, working on my BlackBerry and I accidentally pushed the wrong button—I deleted the whole document!

I had to think about this turn of events for a few days. Maybe I'm not supposed to write a book, I thought. But I couldn't stop thinking about it. Then I remembered my process for music. I have lots of ideas, and when I write them down on paper, I turn my dreams into a tangible vision. With the vision clear on paper, I set goals with deadlines and give the vision momentum. This is how my thoughts become lyrics. So, on July 1, 2011, I went to a store and bought a notebook for 43 cents. I was on tour playing a show in Franklin, Indiana, at the time; I snuck out right after sound check. I took a black Sharpie pen and wrote "Fighter" across the front cover. After all the inner, and outer, battles I've struggled with for so many years, my dreams and aspirations were finally coming to pass; I couldn't stop now.

So, I've written and rewritten this book, over and over. I wrote it out longhand, and then I typed it out, and then I edited it five or six times over. (Hopefully this book will be easier for you to read than it has been for me to write!)

With that thought in mind, the purpose of this book is to inspire you to action. Taking action is key! If I'd never started writing, this book would still just be an idea. I had to manifest it, one word at a time. And by sharing my experiences, my hope is that you will take stock of your dreams and also manifest them into reality. Believe it or not, there is a process that I have used many times to make my dreams come true, a process I want to share. I call it The Anatomy of a Fighter, and it has five parts: Courage, Perseverance, Mindset, Discipline, and Willpower.

Within these pages, I share my story and the precise journey that's brought me to where I am now. I share what I've learned as a result of my mistakes, failures, and successes in life and the music industry. This is not merely head knowledge, but my life knowledge—real-life stories from over the past twelve years, as I've toured in twelve different countries and performed eyeball to eyeball for hundreds of thousands. I will show you how I wrote songs, how I handled rejection, how I maintained a stable lifestyle—and most importantly, how I never gave up.

I've discovered that God is the connector to our dreams, and He is the only one who can truly satisfy us, no matter how high we climb the ladder of success. So, my prayer, as you read this book and the stories on the pages within, is that by exposing my own stories and dreams to the light, it may shed some light on yours.

I always say that if God can do something great with a skate punk from a small town like Pickering, Ontario, I can only imagine what he can do with your life.

"The journey of a thousand miles begins with one step." —Lao Tzu

THE HOUSE WHERE MY FATHER DIED

BEDROOM AS A TEENAGER

Pine Ridge
SECONDARY SCHOOL
2155 LIVERPOOL ROAD

MY HIGH SCHOOL

FIRST NOTES FOR THE FIGHTER BOOK

William Dunbar Public School

MY ELEMENTARY SCHOOL

Composition
FIGHTER

100 Sheets • 200 Pages • Wide Ruled
NORCOM
9½ x 7¾ in • 24.7 x 19.0 cm

town shoes

SKATER PUNKS IN THE MALL

SPEEDY

SCHOOL
BUS
LOADING
ZONE

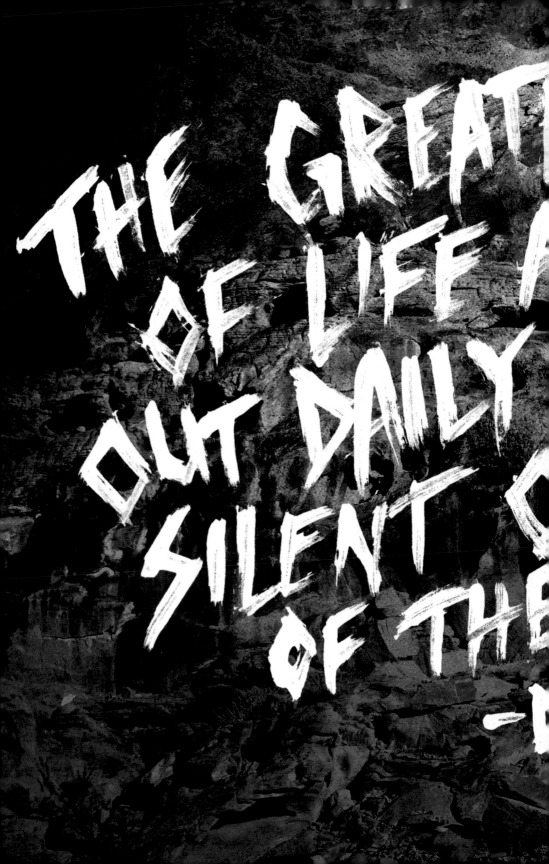

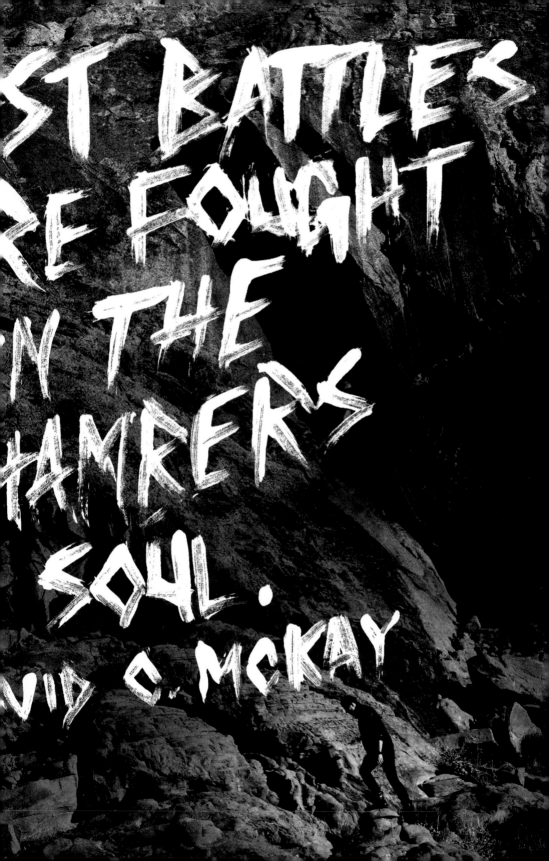

CouRage

Chapter One
COURAGE

I don't like to reflect too much on my early childhood as it was oftentimes filled with uncertainty, loneliness, and fear. Fear would whisper in my ear, preventing me from stepping out by telling me I'd fail. Fear reminded me of my past, so I couldn't live in the present, and would never have a future. Fear is the loudest when you're doing something that matters. And the voice that tells me right now that I have nothing to write about is the same voice that in 2001 told me I've got nothing to sing about. Now, after six albums, 200,000 records sold, and twelve countries toured, I've finally learned not to listen to it.

I've heard that all fear stands for is False Evidence Appearing Real. Fear is an image, or a thought in your mind that seems real, but in reality has no power at all. An illusion. So, to overcome fear, you have to recognize the illusion.

I've named this book Fighter, but I'm not talking about a physical fight in an arena, with an opponent on the other side of the ring ready to throw down. I'm talking about a fight within oneself, with the person staring back at you in the mirror. Most things we worry about never come to pass anyway. We spend so much time replaying negative thoughts in our minds that it paralyzes us. I noticed that I would talk myself out of great ideas before I even tried to use them. Now, as soon as I have a good idea, I act on it immediately and picture myself being successful at it. As the proverb goes, "as a man thinks, so is he." (Proverbs 23:7)."

But I'm no stranger to fear. I can't tell you how many times I skated up to the edge of a staircase to slide down the handrail or "ollie" a set of stairs on my skateboard, and right before I launched, I put my foot down and skidded to a halt. Or how much I've struggled with stage fright. I used to run to the bathroom three or four times before I'd have to go up on stage. One time, at an awards show in Edmonton, Alberta, they announced my name to an empty stage because I'd gotten so excited thinking about what I'd say to the crowd if I won, that I disappeared into the men's room instead of staying backstage like the coordinator told me to. I have a great photo from that night of me standing in front of the men's room holding my award.

Now, after thousands of performances, and numerous speaking gigs in twelve different countries or more, I've built up the courage to get a better handle on my nerves, but they never really go away entirely. I've traveled to Australia, the United States, Canada, Singapore, China, Japan, England, Ireland, Denmark, Sweden, Amsterdam, New Zealand, and Germany. But before every performance, I still have to pinch myself, jump around, or do vocal warm-ups to loosen me up.

Courage isn't something we're born with. We're born with fearlessness, and that's an entirely different thing. Courage has to be built. Like building a muscle, strengthening it by flexing it over and over, and increasing the weight each time. You have to train yourself in courage. The best example I can think of is the open mic nights I used to go to back in Toronto.

"Courage is not the absence of fear. Courage is the willingness to act in spite of my fear." —Michael Hyatt

STEP UP TO THE MIC

Back in the day I had a producer friend named Gerry. He was a real low-key, older hip-hop producer, who had befriended me and started molding me as an artist. He used to help me work on my lyrics, and he came to all my shows. I always say he was like my hip-hop sensei.

One day, after watching me perform, Gerry told me I needed to work on my stage presence. He had a plan. He told me about an open mic at a place called Holy Joes, and one night we drove down there together. I didn't even know if I was going up, but I made sure I dressed fresh, so I'd be confident. It was cold that night, so I had on my brown leather jacket and a beanie, and I threw on some nice cologne. The outside of the building was dark purple, and you had to walk through a club called The Kathedral to get into Holy Joes. We climbed up a winding staircase to the second floor and entered a cozy lounge with a bar, couches against the walls, dimmed lights, and a small stage. A DJ was spinning beats, and the room had a real urban, hip-hop vibe. You could fit about 150 people in there, and it was packed that night.

Some of the best emcees in Toronto gathered here to showcase their talent. Many spent more time and money on their outfits than they did their music, but that's a side note. Most artists wanted to create a buzz about their performance so an A&R guy of a record label would take notice and sign them to a deal. These were the days of hawking your CDs. (Now we live in a world where it's tough to even give your music away, but anyways...) There were two emcees hosting the event—a girl named Tara Chase and a guy named Marvel—plus there was always a DJ spinning.

I went up to the front of the room and put my name down on the sign-up sheet; at some point in the night, they would call me up

25

to perform. As I signed my name, I was so nervous I broke out in a sweat. My hands went clammy, and I started fidgeting. My friend was like, "Are you all right, man? Don't worry, you'll be fine."

There were a lot of people there that night and I didn't know anyone there except Gerry. I was around twenty years old, completely new to the scene, and the only white guy in the room. To make it worse, Toronto was known for its haters. Back in the day, there were rumors that if you sucked as a rapper, they'd pull the fire alarm during your set. If you could make it in Toronto, you could make it anywhere. It wasn't encouraging at all; it kind of freaked me out. A lot of artists, when they're new, feel like they have something to prove, and I assumed people would automatically diss me right away. I had a lot of thoughts that night.

Back then it was all about having a dope verse, not a dope song. You'd go up and spit your dopest verse. So I was sitting there thinking, which one do I choose? The problem is you could have a certain lyric or song in your mind ready to sing, but the DJ could spin a beat that didn't match it. This is where the training comes in, and you have to be able to freestyle, switch it up on the fly. Otherwise, you'll be standing there, staring at the audience staring back at you waiting for you to do something. You do not want to choke.

When they called my name, I nearly fell out of my chair. I got up on stage, and the DJ started spinning a beat. I let it play for a few seconds before I grabbed the mic and kicked a rhyme as hard as I could. Then I put the mic down and started to walk off the stage. I was stage-struck, dizzy with adrenaline, and I just wanted to get to my seat as quickly as possible. I thought, OK, I did it! Now let's get the heck out of here before bottles start flying. But the crowd started cheering. Then I heard Marvel say, "Manafest, get the beep back up here and kick something else. That was hot!"

I thought, wow, they actually liked it! They liked the white boy. And I'm getting an encore! I walked out of there that night with my producer friend feeling taller than the CN Tower. He put his arm around my shoulders, and told me how proud he was—that he would brag about that night for weeks.

I wish all the nights went as great as the first, but that's not the truth.

One time I went to the front to perform, and for some reason, the beat the DJ played caught me off guard. Instead of going right into a dope verse or saying something cool, I said, "Are you feeling the vibe? 'Cause I'm feeling the vibe." I stood there, rocking back and forth like a big white giraffe. I went into an awkward verse, and then sat down where my friend was waiting for me, laughing. I was like, "What? What?" He pointed to two girls sitting in the crowd. They were giggling, mocking me saying, "I'm feeling the vibe, are you feeling the vibe?" I was so embarrassed, but I hung out the rest of the night to watch others perform, network with people, and learn something by watching other artists. One of the greatest assets of touring is seeing so many different live shows and studying what works and what doesn't work with the crowd. It's so much easier when you're just a spectator.

Another night, they called up one of my friends who sang R&B, and he was able to give them a CD so they could play his track. He was a big white guy who dressed kind of like a hillbilly, so the audience was like, "What in God's name is this guy going to do?" Adam Messinger produced the track, so when the beat started, heads were nodding and my friend's voice filled the entire room. Before he was finished, people were on the edge of their seats cheering him on. Marvel was like, "Dang, I thought he was going to play the spoons or something, that beep beep was dope."

After that, I went up every week at Holy Joes—for a year straight. I went up so often that Marvel started introducing me as the "Iron Man" of open mics. I hadn't missed one since it started. Some really dope emcees started coming around, and it took a lot of courage to get up there. After a while I started freestyling, making up rhymes on the spot. People would hold things up and I'd start calling them out. I used Marvel's name in a freestyle bit and earned a lot of respect. Eventually they allowed me to perform there. It was great practice in that volatile environment, where as a performer you have such little control over the show. I didn't know it at the time, but I was building my courage. I was preparing for anything. I was earning my chops.

Open mics kept me sharp. They were the right incubator for my career, and they improved my stage presence eventually. As much as I didn't want to at times, I forced myself back on the stage. I practiced making eye contact with my audience and noticed that if I felt comfortable, then they would, too. My girlfriend, Melanie, worked with me on my rhythm, so I moved more on beat. It was this training that helped me understand how to work a crowd and not lose them. I can now perform a song and, within seconds, know by the facial expressions and body language of the crowd what I need to do to win them over.

As for courage, I remember one night a guy pulled me aside and told me that I may or may not be scared to get up there, but one thing is certain: 90 percent of the people in the crowd would never do it. They would love to do it, but they're too scared. It's true. If you can do something that the majority of people cannot do—what are you waiting for? Get up and just do it.

"The important thing is this: to be able at any moment to sacrifice what we are for what we could become." —Charles Dubois

I QUIT

I can still see myself sitting at my desk, reading and rereading the email I had typed up to my boss asking to have a meeting about my resignation. I looked up at the office ceiling, closed my eyes—and with all the weight of the world in my fingers coming down on the keyboard, I hit Send.

Quitting my job took a different kind of courage.

I was in my early twenties, working as a network engineer (aka computer nerd), making around $70,000 a year, with a comfy office and full benefits. I was still living at home at that time, so I wasn't worrying about rent. I had already started a music career by then, so on the weekends and most weeknights I performed, and by day I'd work with computers and daydream about playing music full time, until it became a daily habit.

I'd just gotten signed to Tooth & Nail Records and I thought I had built up my music career enough to make the jump. According to plan, I had gone from working five days a week, to four days, to three days and so on, taking off Mondays and Fridays to play shows. Finally, I requested a leave of absence from my job to go on tour for a month. My boss had always been supportive, but asking for a month off took a lot of guts. My cash flow fluctuated as I whittled down my working days and funneled money into my music.

I didn't know how I was going to pay the bills. I thought, what happens if nobody likes my music? Am I ever going to be good enough? What if I quit, fail, and they won't give me my job back? Do I really have what it takes?

Then I got some advice from a good friend. He said, "You don't want to be forty years old looking back at your life wondering, 'What if?'" What if you never quit your job? What if you never called that girl? What if you never went to college? What if, what if, and what if?

I worked out my income quickly on a piece of paper, and called my lawyer, asking him how much I would need to make it work. I would have to start touring full time. Then I called my manager and told him my monthly budget and the amount of income I needed to cover my bills. He said OK, cool. I was so green back then. I had no idea how cutthroat and unforgiving this industry was. I was going to be a rap star. I wanted it so bad. I prayed with my wife long and hard. I would soon find out just how much I was going to need those prayers.

Faith is taking action when common sense says no.

After I sent my resignation letter, my boss scheduled an in-person meeting with me at his house. He asked me to leave for a little while and come back to work part-time. I told him how much I appreciated his offer but I politely declined. I didn't know how good I had it. Not only were they paying me well, but they promoted me quickly, and they understood my passion for music. I remember one Christmas the Vice President of the company bought me Eminem's greatest hits as a show of solidarity; when I opened the gift that was sitting on my desk at 8 a.m. in the morning and saw who it was from, it blew me away. But I guess it was my rebel side, the skater punk in me fighting against the suits that was driving me away. I still wanted to do music.

And from that point forward, I put my finances in the hands of people I barely knew. I went on the road. I had a manager who never really believed in my music, and people made promises that were never kept. I went deep into debt in the process. But I also learned about the music business, I traveled the world, and I figured out how the machine worked. The music industry, whether Christian or not, is like the NFL. You're the quarterback, and better have your game face on or you're gonna' get run over. There was so much holding me back, and it took me years to figure it out. But when I look back,

I know if I hadn't had the courage to get out there and try something new I wouldn't be where I am today.

Now more than nine years later, I'm sitting in my house in California writing this book and thanking God I stepped out and had the courage to see it through. So many times, I wanted to quit and go back to that job; so many times, I cried when it got tough. So many times, I second-guessed if it was the right decision. I'd be staying in some stranger's home, on the road with a backpack full of CDs and a microphone, begging people to love my music. Or playing sweaty, nasty festivals in the middle of summer, wondering what I was doing, when I had left an air-conditioned office and people who loved working with me. Pushing through all that crap. It's not sexy.

Creating your own path is a lot of hard work and it's lonely. It takes courage to have a vision, especially when other people can't see it. The label couldn't see it. My manager couldn't see it. I was just a white rapper from Canada; they didn't see potential there, or sales. I wasn't marketable in their eyes. I watched them put money behind other artists, and make the important calls—all the things I wanted them to do for me, but didn't. The label wasn't pushing me properly, I didn't have any radio hits, and some of my songs just weren't there. I had to push myself and pull others along with me. And that gets tiring. But you get to learn a lot about yourself. At what point is there not enough courage left to keep going? Where's your breaking point? Now I ask myself, what do I see now that I didn't see five years ago? And how would someone else live my life if they were me? That way I can find new visions to propel myself forward.

Courage takes commitment.

When I was skating, I used to roll up with my wheels right on the edge of a staircase or gap, shouting, "Come on, just do it!" and seeing myself in my mind standing at the top. I'd scream, throw my board, spit, and try anything just to stir myself up. Eventually my friends with the camera would shout, "Stop being such a wimp!" The problem is I had to just commit. No plan B, just go for it. I'd pray, meditate, and catch my breath, but once my wheels left the pavement and I flew off the stairs, I was committed. If I managed to even come close, without hurting myself, all the fear was gone. Each attempt became easier and easier. It's our fear of the unknown, or what we think might happen that holds us back.

I didn't ask permission. I didn't say, "Should I be a musician?" If I'd based my decision on the approval of others, it wouldn't have been enough. I never asked anyone but God, and he helped me overcome fear. I just know that if it's your passion, then it comes from the right source, so do it. Courage has to come from inside, and approval has to come from a source larger than yourself. Don't ask others to approve your dreams or set your goals for you; by doing that you're giving up your God given gift of choice. So, all I have to say is whatever your dream is, do it, despite what everyone else says, or you'll be the one staring back at your life wondering, what if, what if…what if? It's at the bottom where it's crowded, but there is plenty of room at the top.

HOLY JOE'S OPEN MIC LOCATION, TORONTO, ON

IN THE STUDIO WITH
ADAM MESSINGER

FIRST PRESS PHOTO

DJ VERSATILE SPINNING AT WEST 49 SKATE SHOP

STARTED DATING MELANIE

ACTION STEPS:

1). Sometimes I've let other people's opinions hold me back. Write down two things you've always wanted to do, but haven't followed through on because you were afraid of what someone else would think.

2). Write down two actions you could take right now that would not only push you out of your comfort zone, but would also put you a step closer toward your dreams. Dream big, but break it down into smaller, manageable steps. For instance, what I do is write down each step and post it somewhere where I can see it every day, like on the fridge, or on my computer, or a bedroom wall. (Suggestions: make that phone call, send in that resume, write that lyric, book that appointment, go to the gym.)

PERSEVERANCE

Chapter two
PERSEVERANCE

"That's it. I'm doing it," I told myself. One last try.

I was in downtown Toronto, wearing nothing but my white-and-gray camouflage cargo pants, dripping with sweat. My friend had been holding the camera for more than thirty minutes while I tried to land the same trick over and over. I'd gotten a few tricks on film that day—a nollie kickflip and a 180 heelflip—but the switch frontside 180 kickflip was the one I really wanted. Sometimes my left foot would be on the board, but my right foot slipped off. I just couldn't land it. I loved filming skateboarding videos (I still do), but I was aware of the risks. We were running out of time; any second the security guard might come and kick us out.

I rolled up to the stairs, focused and determined to land it. My wheels left the marble concrete, and midair I noticed my board wasn't rotating all the way around, but it was too late—I'd already committed. I landed primo, all my weight on the side of the board, with the truck's axle digging into my left foot. I immediately fell to the ground in pain. A few seconds later, I got to my feet and limped up the stairs, thinking I'd be OK. I wanted to give it one more try.

I got back on my board, but I couldn't handle the pain. I tried walking it off, but it hurt too much. For fifteen minutes I sat there waiting, looking up at the sky, hoping and praying the pain would go away. Every time I got up and tried to put weight on my foot, I fell over in agony.

Our skateboarding session was obviously over. I had to sit on my skateboard while my friend pushed me back to the train station to go home. It really ticked me off. Toronto is similar to New York with its crazy drivers, so I sat on my board cradling my busted foot, trying not to get run over by a car. Once we got on the train, we replayed the tape and watched my trick on the camera. We cracked lots of jokes about me falling. I wish I could show you the clip from that video of the fall that literally changed my destiny, but I accidentally taped over it. That's how little importance I gave it at the time. The way I saw it, it was just a bad fall; I'd be better tomorrow, ready to skate flat ground at least.

The next day when I rolled out of bed and put my feet on the ground. a sharp pain shot through my left foot. I fell back onto the bed, grabbed my foot, and said, "You've got to be kidding me!" I limped around the house all day, but I was still optimistic that my foot would heal up fast. A few days later I could walk on it, and I did get back on my skateboard. But every time I tried to do a trick, the painful pressure on my left foot stopped me.

Finally, my mom convinced me to go to the doctor, but I only went as a last resort. I remember sitting in the office for what felt like eternity, waiting for the physician to come in and tell me what was wrong. After examining my foot, he told me it wasn't broken, but there must be internal bruising. The way he said it, it sounded like no big deal. It's a bruise! I would be fine as long as I didn't skate on it for a week.

One week turned into two, and then two weeks turned into three, and then a month—and I still wasn't better.

It was at that moment I felt like my dreams were completely wiped out. Everything I'd worked for had fallen apart right in front of my face. Forget about moving to California and becoming a pro, or skating in contests, being in videos, having my own board and shoe design—all of that was gone. Already, I'd skipped school, dumped girlfriends, and spent every last dollar on skateboarding. I had just graduated high school, but I hadn't even applied to any colleges. For the first time I felt fear: if I couldn't skate, what would I do?

All the rage rose up in me and I threw things across the room. I spit, cursed, and blamed God and everyone else but myself. I remember saying the rudest thing to my aunt for no reason one time. I wasn't a nice person to be around. I hated my life.

"Speak when you are angry, and you will make the best speech you will ever regret." —Ambrose Bierce

PROBLEMS ARE A SIGN OF LIFE

Poor little white boy from suburbia who had skateboarding taken away. Normally, I'd go skate around the city when I was angry, but I couldn't even do that. I started thinking of all the terrible things I could do. I thought about drinking, or doing drugs, but I knew it wouldn't make me feel better. I felt like I'd just fallen into a dark pit, and it took me months to climb out of it.

I thought about my father, who had committed suicide; when things got tough, he didn't know how to handle it. I can't say I've never thought about it, because the truth is when I was younger the idea ran through my mind a lot. At one point, I even saw a psychiatrist to help me talk out some of the problems. Suicide is a permanent solution to a temporary problem. There will always be problems, no matter what stage of life you're at.

Dr. Norman Vincent Peale said, "Problems are a sign of life."

The more problems you've got, the more alive you are. Many people run from problems instead of facing them. It's those that stick it out in the hard times and remain steady who grow. Suicide isn't the answer; your life is worth living, and we need you!

"I may have been in a dark place, but I wasn't a failure until I start blaming other people for my problems." —Manafest

DON'T GIVE UP

When I think of perseverance, I think of the story of the tortoise and the hare, and how slow and steady wins the race. I think of marathon runners. I think about the kid whose parents gave him a brand new nice car, versus the kid that worked all summer for it and bought it himself. I think of my widowed mom, who selflessly raised two kids on her own. I think about getting bad news, falling down, negative thinking, and failing to achieve overly high expectations. And I especially think about being forced to rethink the entire strategy of your life due to unavoidable circumstances, like an injury.

In the last chapter, I talked about having the courage to start, and now I'm talking about something much harder—how to keep going.

In my opinion, the reason you don't hear about some successful people for a very long time is because they were working so much! I used to tell myself that when I toured with a certain band, I'd made it. Or if I sold a certain number of albums, I'd arrived. But my personal definition of success kept changing and so I kept striving for more, growing and getting better every day. I just kept going.

There aren't many at the top because so many people give up along the way. Sometimes people tell me they quit music because they had to get a job…I say they quit because they couldn't handle it. It isn't mean; it's the truth. They wanted security, not success. And sometimes success takes a very long time.

Take my music career, for example. This is how it started.

The months following the accident, I just tried to stay busy and maybe meet a new girl— anything to keep my mind off skateboarding. One night I was at a youth Christmas banquet at a church I'd been attending; it was a formal dinner set up with white linen–dressed tables facing the front of the room where a stage with speakers and a set of turntables stood in the middle. After dinner was served, the lights dimmed, and suddenly a hip-hop performance exploded on the stage. I'd never seen a show like that before. The lights were flashing, and the guys were running around the stage rapping—they looked like they were having a blast. My friends and I started dancing and throwing our hands up—some dudes were even break-dancing. I was blown away. When the show was over, I introduced myself to the rap group and hung out with them.

They were much older than me, but they put up with the dozens of questions I threw at them that night because I wanted to learn more about hip-hop. One night, they invited me over to listen to some records at their house, and they showed me how to write rap lyrics. They were buying tons of artists' singles on vinyl that had only one or two songs on each side, plus the instrumental. They used the instrumental to write and record their own lyrics and songs. When they wanted to record, they'd have a record player plugged into a mixer, with a microphone. They'd hit Play on the record player and record onto the tape deck, rapping songs into the mic. Then we'd play it back on the tape deck to hear how it sounded.

I flipped through their entire collection of vinyl looking for a song with an instrumental track that I liked, and started writing lyrics. There were so many albums and artists I'd never even heard of—it was a whole new world. After this night, I started carrying a pocket-sized notebook with me at all times to write my rhymes in.

This was my introduction to hip-hop, and it was inspiring. My first introduction to music, on the other hand, was a different story.

THERE'S NO "F" IN MUSIC

Ever since I can remember I liked music. Our family always encouraged listening and singing along to music, as long as it was positive. At night, I'd lay in bed with my ghetto blaster next to me as I fell asleep, playing Michael Jackson, the Beach Boys, or Alvin and the Chipmunks. I'd scan the radio at night for my favorite songs, and when I'd find one I liked, I'd hit Record on the deck and tape it onto a cassette. I remember going to my uncle's house for Christmas and being in awe of his giant vinyl collection. He'd make me mixtapes of songs to take home with me. When I was in third grade, I was the first kid who asked the teacher if I could bring my music to play during gym class. I felt pretty cool knowing I was the one who brought the party tunes while we ran around during our warm-ups. One of the songs we'd all sing along to while running was Jerry Lee Lewis's "Great Balls of Fire."

The first time I picked up an instrument, it was the trumpet, in fifth grade. I can still feel the excitement in the classroom as all the instruments were pulled out and the rush of synergy in the place as kids moved around. I remember a lot of the guys fighting over who got to play the drums. They allowed only one student out of twenty-seven to play drums, and my friend was picked over the rest of us because he owned a set at home. The only instruments available then were clarinets, saxophones, trombones, flutes, and trumpets. No guitars, basses, or turntables.

At the time I listened to a lot of Nirvana and Guns N' Roses. I loved the rebellion and attitude in their songs. Had my music teacher come into class with a guitar and started playing "Smells like Teen Spirit" by Nirvana, the students' faces would have lit up instantly. I would have been like a fat kid and his cake, practicing all through the night, learning every riff to every song on the Nevermind album. I wish that was the case, but it wasn't. Instead, our teacher acted like a drill sergeant, standing in front of her militia of sixth graders, all sitting in perfect rows. During test time, we'd sit silent with our sheet music in front of us, while one by one she would go down the line signaling each student to play. I remember one day it was my turn to play, and I saw my classmates giggling and passing around notes that said, "It looks like Chris is French kissing his trumpet." I was so embarrassed. Sweat dripped down my forehead and my fingers shook as I pressed one wrong note after the next. I felt like bending that trumpet over my knee, twisting it into a slinky, and smashing it through the window.

In that class we weren't taught how to express ourselves or our emotions, and we were never allowed to experiment. We didn't write poems or song lyrics either. It was completely one-dimensional. So I learned the trumpet, and was forced to play music I didn't enjoy. I just couldn't get good at it. I even borrowed a trumpet from my friend Bruce so I could practice at home, but I wasn't any good. Now I see why it was so easy for someone like me to slip through the cracks when I didn't immediately connect with what they were teaching. Before the year was up, I had tried and failed to play every instrument available, with the saxophone being the worst experience.

Even the theory of music wasn't becoming clear to me. One day my teacher pulled me aside and said, "Maybe music just isn't your thing." (What kind of a teacher says that to a kid?) I barely passed the course with a 52 percent, and they gave it to me just so I wouldn't fail the whole grade. From then on, I never thought about playing music again. In fact, I was bitter about it. I can recall walking through the hallways of my high school and the sounds of the big band playing making my insides shudder. Now I just laugh because I've had what many would consider a successful music career. It's amazing how your whole life can be going in one direction, and in a blink of an eye, the gears shift and move completely the opposite way.

"You build on failure. You use it as a stepping-stone. Close the door on the past. You don't try to forget the mistakes, but you don't dwell on it. You don't let it have any of your energy, or any of your time, or any of your space." —Johnny Cash

PAY TO PLAY

I get funny looks when I tell my friends or other artists that I'm not getting paid for a show. But their eyes really pop out of their sockets when I tell them that not only am I not getting paid, but I also cover my own travel expenses. This is how the music industry works; sometimes the only way to get on a larger tour is to buy on. To this day I still buy on to bigger tours, and now bands are buying onto mine. Depending on the tour, it can be worth it, and you make a lot of new fans.

On one tour, I paid $150 per show to the headlining band for a fifteen-minute slot, but it didn't include transportation, so I still had to pay another band to let me catch a ride in their van, on top of covering my own hotel costs. This was before I had a band and I traveled solo, so many nights I slept on hotel room floors to save money. To make matters worse, there were five bands on that bill, so we had very little time for setup, and I had to perform one or two songs in between the set changes. Every night guys would disrupt my performance by coming onstage to plug in cables. They'd even bump into me while moving their gear around. It was absolutely ridiculous.

Another time I bought on to another tour many years later, and paid $1000 a night, plus covered my own travel, hotel, and bandmates. (But unlike earlier ones, this tour was very successful and I would do it again in a heartbeat because I got to reach so many more fans, and I was treated like a professional.)

If you can imagine it, right before I went on that tour, the company I'd quit called me to offer me my job back with an even higher salary! The easy way out was staring me right in the face, like a golden apple on a platter. Fortunately, I knew if I took the job, I would be giving up too soon. I decided to take the road less traveled!

2 Corinthians 12:9 — "My grace is sufficient for you, for My power is made perfect in weakness."

SLEEPING BY THE SIDE OF THE ROAD LESS TRAVELED

I will never forget my first tour across the United States with my friend Jeff Goring, driving from Toronto, Canada to Seattle, Washington. We were stuffed into a 2006 Pontiac Vibe along with all our luggage, merchandise, and pillows, like a tightly packed can of tuna. We had no GPS, just a map we'd picked up at a gas station and the road signs to guide our journey. Neither of us had ever done anything like this before, so we were super stoked!

We drove into the sunset, watching the sky change colors on the horizon. We were like Batman and Robin on a mission into the unknown, leaving the Great White North and heading into the land of Stars and Stripes. We took lots of pictures of the state signs, and we had lots of time to do so, because I think we took more U-turns and pulled off at more exits to ask for directions than on any other road trip I've taken. The music was blasting inside the car and kept the adrenaline pumping through our veins as we talked about the future.

By 1 a.m. of the first day, we pulled over to the side of the road to sleep. We'd gone as far as we could and we were exhausted. It was a dark, dusty road with no light except for the moon. Every time a massive eighteen-wheeler sped past us, the car would shake, but I managed to find a comfortable spot with my pillow wedged against the driver's side door and was just about to fall asleep. That's when Jeff started moving around. He shifted position every ten minutes! Finally, the racket he was making was too much; I lost my cool and yelled, "You've got one minute to find a comfortable spot and go to sleep!" This was our first day, and the first of many frustrating moments we'd have while we lived together on the road for the next month.

On this trip we played lots of hot, nasty festivals surrounded by crowds with tattooed arms and spiky Mohawks. We got a flat tire, got stranded in the desert, and yet we still managed to make it to our last stop in Quincy, California, without killing each other.

This part of my career definitely tested my perseverance, my patience, and my friendships. The worst memory I have of touring was in New Mexico playing a show. When I landed, nobody was there to pick me up, and I didn't bring a jacket, because I thought it would be warm, but it wasn't. I ended up sleeping on a cold bench for hours waiting for the promoter to come get me. When I did finally get picked up I was a shivering, starving mess. The driver took me to get breakfast at a smoke-filled café to nourish my scrawny frame. When I finally arrived at the venue, my bandmates decided to play a joke on me; they hid all my merchandise in the van and trailer so I couldn't find it. I was only getting paid $35 dollars for each show, and without my merchandise, I had no other way of making money. After searching for my stuff, and questioning every bandmate, I gave up and wandered into a room by myself and turned out the lights. I broke down and cried like a baby.

I once heard a friend say to a band, "If you want to see if you're a tight-knit band, go on tour together." After the first tour, groups either break up or continue on for a lifetime.

ALMOST THERE

We headed to our final show on the tour in Quincy at the JoshuaFest. We pulled into a campground a day early, and since there were no hotels, the parking area of the campground was our only option. Jeff had started calling me Grumpyfest. He decided to make his bed outside with the chipmunks instead of spending another night crammed in the car with me.

Jeff took his sleeping bag and pillow and lay down on the grassy floor under a starry night sky. It was quiet, and we were both fast asleep, until about 3 a.m., when he woke up to a clicking noise. It was the sound of the sprinkler system going off. Within seconds, Jeff was soaked. I had locked the car door before nodding off, so Jeff spent five minutes banging on the car, trying to wake me. He was not amused.

Despite this, we played a great show on the main stage at JoshuaFest, and after signing autographs we jumped into the car. I squeezed the steering wheel tightly. My eyes were focused on the task at hand—driving sixteen hours straight to Vancouver, BC. I was amped because I was going to see my wife for the first time in weeks; we were just recently married.

When I saw Melanie in Vancouver, it was like the heavens opened up, music started playing, and we ran to each other in slow motion, like a scene from a movie. I shared all the stories with her about being on the road, and we had some good laughs. Sometimes the reward for perseverance is just being able to see your loved ones at the end of the journey.

STRONGER

I remember one time, early in my music career after I'd quit my job, walking home from the grocery store with Melanie in a snowstorm because we had no car. Our fingers were bright red as we carried heavy bags of groceries back to our apartment. We had to count almost every item we purchased so we wouldn't go over our budget, in case there wasn't enough money in our account; it was so bad, we had to laugh. We knew one day we'd look back and say, "See, we didn't give up, and look what God has done." We knew God had big things in store for us.

As the scripture says, "He who is faithful with little will be ruler over much." (Luke 16:10).

We just kept going.

THE MAN WHO WOULDN'T STOP

I once heard a story of a sixty-one-year-old Australian man by the name of Cliff Young who entered an ultramarathon in Australia that was over 500 miles long, from Sydney to Melbourne. The day of the event, he walked into the registration area and was mistaken for a spectator, but when he received his racing number, it was clear he intended to compete. Critics thought it was a joke. Cliff Young told them that he was a farmer, and was accustomed to running down his sheep night after night, sometimes running for three days straight to keep up with them. He was confident he would not only enter the race, but win it. The younger contestants thought they'd all leave this sixty-one-year-old in the dust.

The race began, and sure enough, the marathoners took off in a dash, leaving Cliff Young behind. But after a couple of nights, some of the runners stopped to rest, while Cliff ran on. He shuffled on and on, keeping a steady pace, denying himself sleep for five days, and maneuvering himself into first place to win the race. Cliff Young became a world-class athlete and a national hero in 1983, at sixty-one. Some of the runners, who were pulled off the race for medical treatment, gave interviews from the hospital, hiding under the sheets, and essentially saying the same thing: How do you beat a man who doesn't stop?

When I heard the comment, 'how do you beat a man that doesn't stop?' it rang true in my heart and did something to me. Whenever I think I can't go anymore, God whispers in my ear, "Keep going, boy. I'm with you." And I get up and go again.

PRESSING ON

What do you do when you're knocked down again and again? What do you do when your dreams start to fade? Do you quit and say forget it?

These were the questions I asked myself.

The longer I stayed down the harder it was to get back up, that's why I pulled myself up and reached for another dream. Perseverance is not taking no for an answer. Perseverance is knocking on the door and if no one answers, then kicking it down. Perseverance is reaching, while others are falling. Perseverance is getting back up, again and again.

I don't know where you're at today or what your story is, but can I dare you to take another step? Can I dare you to keep moving and give it another shot?

I'm living my dream because I persevered. Longevity is a key component to success. I had to reinvent myself around playing music, instead of skating. I had to push through financial hardship and put in the hard work before I got my reward. I always wanted to live in

California and skate. I'm not skating for a career, but I'm definitely in California, skating. It took me twelve years for my dream to manifest, but I'm standing in it right now. And that's an amazing thing.

"I am not the smartest or most talented person in the world, but I succeeded because I keep going, and going, and going." —Sylvester Stallone

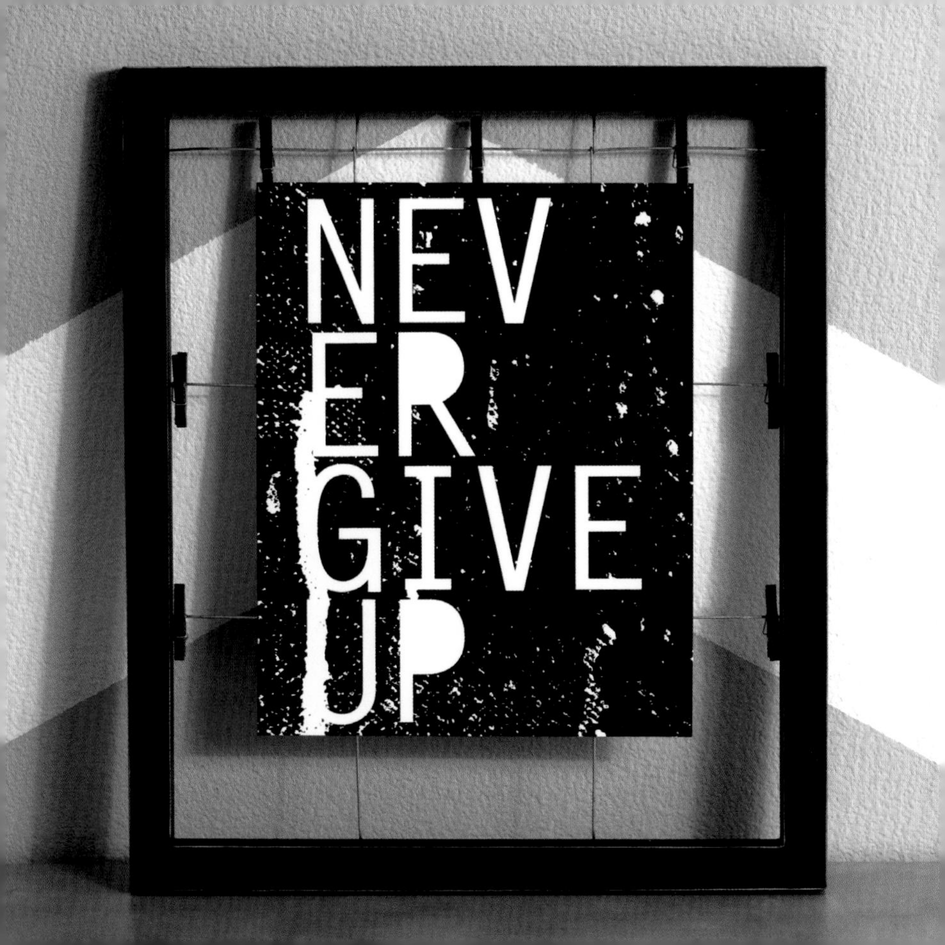
NEV
ER
GIVE
UP

EVER SKATE COMPETITION IN PICKERING, ONTARIO

"FIRE IN THE KITCHEN" VIDEO MASK, PART OF LIVE SH

IN THE MUD, FIGHTER MUSIC VIDEO

TOWER RECORDS, TOKYO

FREESTYLING WITH OBJECTS FROM CROWD

RECORDING ON TOUR IN A LOCKER ROOM

OFFICIAL "FIGHTER" SHIRT

"THE CHASE" ALBUM LAUNCHES IN JAPAN

ACTION STEPS:

1). Life doesn't always go the way we planned. When I was 18 years old my skateboarding career came to a halt, if you were in similar circumstances and your career took a sharp turn or suddenly ended—what would you do?

2). My biggest challenge right now is writing my first book. What is the biggest challenge in your life at the moment? Now list three ways you can respond positively to it.

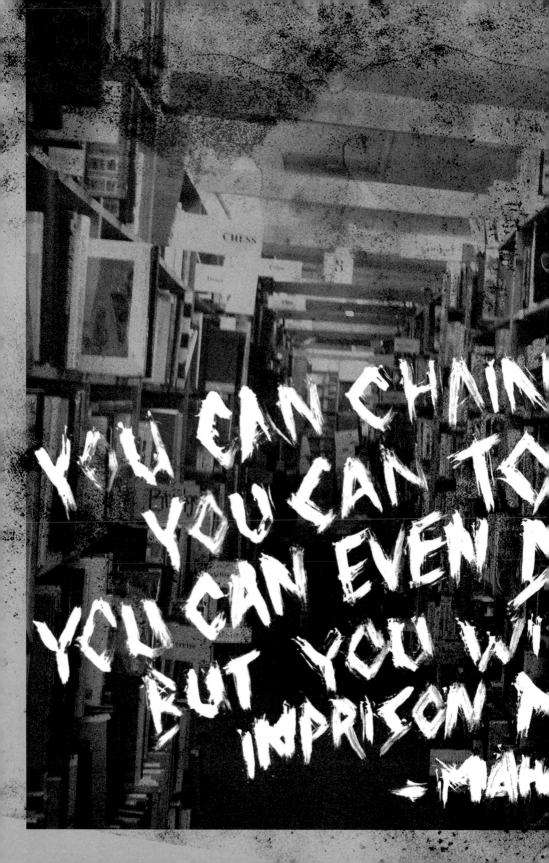

Fighter's Mind Set

Chapter Three
FIGHTER'S MIND SET

If we can get our thinking right, then we can get our actions right; and if we get our actions right, we can overcome any obstacle. I heard Creflo Dollar say, "You sow a thought, and you reap an action; you sow an action, and you reap a habit; you sow a habit, and you reap a character; you sow a character and you reap a destiny." It all begins with our thoughts and there's a big difference between our minds responding, and reacting.

In the song "Glory" I talk about feeling so discouraged that I don't even want to leave my house. I write about fearful thoughts wrestling me down to the ground and holding me captive. *I'm not scared of dying / maybe scared of failing / so I stop trying / evil thoughts start prevailing.*

I can't write songs when my mind is dwelling on negativity, or filled with the wrong thoughts. After you create a hit song, you find yourself staring at the next blank piece of paper with doubts, wondering, Can I do it again? Creating art is scary; no one wants to be laughed at. It is so important to have a strong, healthy mind. One of the scriptures I share a lot when I do public speaking is 2 Timothy 1:7, which says that we weren't born with a spirit of fear, but of power, love, and of a sound mind.

I need to stay positive if I want to handle the challenges I get dealt each day. If I freaked out every time something went wrong, I'd damage a lot of relationships—and I'd have quit years ago. The channel I chose to get me through those doubtful moments is God, so I find prayer helpful. I noticed that what I expose my mind to greatly affects my thoughts. Someone once told me that just like we need to fill our bodies with certain foods so they operate at an efficient level, the same goes for our minds and spirits. There's a connection there.

When I wake up in the morning, I always try to put something inspirational in front of my eyes and into my ears before anything else can come in (like a negative email or a piece of bad news). Lately, I've been getting up at 8:30 a.m. (that's early for a rapper) to jog around my street for a half hour; I put in my earbuds and have something inspirational playing on my iPhone the entire time to pump me up. Running gets my body motivated, but the messages I listen to put my thinking on the right path, too. As my old boss used to say whenever he would see me working out in the office gym, "Healthy body, healthy mind!"

MY TRIGGERS

I don't know what it is about hotels, but some nights I just can't get to sleep. My mind won't shut off. I'll be lying there thinking of inspiring ideas for music, dreaming up different plans and hopes for the future. I get stirred up from the show, because I love what I do. Other times I'll be stressed out, running numbers, worried about how I'm going to pay my team or my bills. I'll tell you, the financial pressure never goes away entirely, no matter how successful you are. Or other times I'll come back after a great night in which kids approached me to tell me how much I've changed their lives, and I sold lots of merchandise, took photos, and signed autographs, but for some reason I'm not focusing on the good things that happened. I'll focus on the negative. Why didn't such-and-such happen? Why didn't I do this better? I'm not good enough.

When I'm tired my mind blows things out of proportion. I start thinking, "Oh, woe is me!" What I really need is a good night's sleep. Unfortunately, when you're on the road as much as I am, that's not always going to happen.

Perspective is entirely in your thoughts, and thoughts have triggers. A trigger can be anything, like when we hear certain songs on the radio, visit certain places (hotel rooms, for instance?), or watch a particular movie. The key is to identify our triggers and counteract them with positive-thought catalysts.

A good way to get my mind to shift from negative to positive is to say out loud that I'm thankful. God says in Philipians 4:8, to think on things that are lovely, peaceful, and joyful. There's a reason for that. I've experienced it firsthand. I used to say things to myself like, "I suck." Or "I can never get it right." And the list goes on and on. I changed my words to, "I can do this. Do it now." Or "I'm going to make it." By saying certain words and speaking with faith, these have had a direct correlation to what I'm thinking, and the results I get are mind-blowing. Like General Raymond J. Reeves said, "Stop thinking about ways things can't be done, and start thinking about how they can be done."

Another one of my biggest triggers is criticism. Depending on whom it's coming from, a negative comment from someone I respect can hit my heart and mind in more impactful ways than a random post on Facebook or YouTube. I had a friend who used to get caught up in all the online criticism; he was wasting his time. I told him to move on.

Just keep creating. I don't like to read reviews of my music anymore, whether they're good or bad. I just want to focus on the mission.

Learning how to handle rejection and process it was a big challenge. Rejection emails from labels, festivals booking another band instead of yours, playing a show and watching people walk past your booth to buy another band's CD and T-shirt instead of yours…How do you handle that? You can't take it personally, but that's something they don't teach you in school. It takes courage to make art and put it out there for people to love or hate, or even worse—ignore. I heard a homeless person say once that it isn't as hard to get rejected with a flat-out no as it is when people pretend you don't even exist. And that's exactly what the music industry feels like: putting your heart out there and getting no response.

When I took that leave of absence from my job I was doing high school assemblies, playing in front of 500 to 1,000 people, and I wasn't a seasoned performer. I would allow my immature self to dictate how I felt about a show and small things would totally wreck my thinking and ruin my whole day. At one of those assemblies some guys tossed pennies at me from the crowd. It really discouraged me. I went home and dyed my hair black that night. I let a couple of haters ruin it for all the people who liked me. Here, people were coming up to me after the show to tell me it totally changed their life, CDs were flying off the tables, and I knew I shouldn't allow the little things to get to me, but in the beginning it would happen all the time.

To be entirely transparent, which is the aim of writing this book, I find myself pointing an angry finger at the record label a lot nowadays, too. That's a dangerous one. An extensive dry spell of tour bookings when your main income comes from playing shows can trigger a lot of negative thoughts. "Why aren't they doing anything?" "Why don't they care about me?" "How can I pay my bills like this?"

Financial stress can send anyone into the blackest mood, and if you don't know how to battle those thoughts, you could get stuck in there.

FIGHT THOUGHTS

The problem is that you can't fight thoughts with thoughts. You have to fight thoughts with words, and specifically God's words. One of my favorite books is The Power of Positive Thinking by Dr. Norman Vincent Peale. He tells some amazing stories of how he has prescribed God's word to people to speak over themselves, and it has changed their lives.

I had a friend that I met through an organization called Big Brothers Big Sisters after the death of my father. I'll never forget him listening to a tape recording in the car of his voice saying, "I like myself. I like myself. I'm going to have a good day today. I'm going to have a good day today." I remember thinking that was so silly, but now I know the impact of speaking positive words. We all talk to ourselves, sometimes out loud or sometimes in our head. There have been dozens of times I've walked around my house talking to myself. Yes, this sounds crazy, but we all do it from time to time. Some of my best thinking has come from bantering back and forth in my head, or out loud to myself.

Affirmations can really make a big difference. Knowing there's a plan for my life, knowing I'm doing God's work, grabbing scriptures and reading them out loud when I'm battling negativity—I realize that it's a lot like pumping myself up for a fight. The battlefield is in the mind, and you have to stir yourself up with words. You have to want to win.

Take the lyrics to my song "Bring the Ruckus" as an example. It's a real anthemic war chant: *You can try, but you won't take me down / I'm standing on my ground / as all the fear inside me fades away.*

You gotta be armed and ready for war, mentally, because if you're mind is defeated, then you've lost the fight before you step in the ring.

I have to get into the right mindset before I can sit down and write a song. When I wrote the song about my father's death, "Where Are You," I was sitting in a hotel room in Salt Lake City. There was an earthquake that night. I had to replay a lot of intense memories in my mind to get into the zone, and by the time the words started flowing, I was crying. The same goes when you're writing an aggressive song. I perform it for myself first to work up the emotions, so that my lyrics come across the way I want them to. You can't whisper, "I'M A FIGHTER!!!" That's why I lock myself up in my studio when I do my songwriting…so I can do embarrassing things, by myself, as much as I want.

These days I carry a journal around with me all the time in which I write positive quotes, lyrics, scriptures, and the things God speaks to me about. My wife bought me my first one as a gift in 2006, and it's become an amazing tool for me to get my thoughts out. I filled that first one up and now am on my second one. Whenever I'm down, I flip through the pages, reading all the positive quotes inside. It's filled with so much inspiration that within minutes I can sing a solo with a whole different outlook. It lifts my emotions and boosts my self-image.

Also, who you hang out with affects your thoughts. Hang out with people who want to win, who see a positive angle on life. Don't hang out with the complainers. At the start of our adult lives, we just have the friends we grew up with. But from then on, we choose our friends. So choose wisely.

Before I perform, and definitely before I speak, I like to clear my mind and get my thoughts together. I can't be chatting with dozens of people and have an in-depth conversation with them right before

I hit the stage, or I will lose my focus. I used to think that renewing my mind was a one-time event. Now, I realize if I don't renew my mind daily, it gets negative.

Yes, Manafest sometimes has contaminated thoughts, but when that happens, I say, "That's not my thought." I'll say this out loud, "My thoughts are peaceful, joyful, loving, and I will think on these things. I have the mind of Christ. I'm more than a conqueror. I walk in love, not in fear." Now, I challenge thoughts when they try to enter, and I guard my mind like an angel standing in front of the gates of heaven. I don't just let any thought come in and try to root itself in my mind and wreak havoc. I pull that sucker out of there and throw it in the trash where it belongs.

Romans 12:2 — "Don't copy the behavior and customs of this world, but let God transform you into a new person by changing the way you think. Then you will learn to know God's will for you, which is good and pleasing and perfect." (NLT)

THOUGHTS ARE BELIEFS

"You must learn a new way to think before you can master a new way to be." —Marianne Williamson

Our thoughts are our beliefs. How we see and experience the world, how we view ourselves and the people in our lives, is greatly shaped by how observant we are, and the way we describe things in our minds. Here are some examples of ideas I had about myself, the world, and the music biz, ideas I had to find new definitions for as I grew and matured.

The world is a big place, and every time I visit a new country and realize there is more than one way of living, it blows my mind. It challenges my mental flexibility to see people enjoying their lives differently. For example, I couldn't get a hot drink to go when I was in France. I had to slow down if I wanted a hot drink; I had to stop, sit, and enjoy my tea instead of running around town with it. I'm sure I was seen walking down the street wolfing down my chicken kebab wrap or whatever, before I noticed that nobody walks around eating in a lot of other countries. They were probably thinking, "That crazy American (or Canadian) doesn't know how to relax and enjoy his food!"

Another big definition change was when I came to realize that I'm a leader—but I'm not Superman. I can't be everything to everyone, and no matter how much I want to, I can't please everybody. But when I started hiring band members, putting music out there, and stepping out in front of larger and larger crowds, I had to admit it: I'm a leader. Truthfully, though, it still freaks me out sometimes. Leadership comes with a lot of responsibility.

Also, I used to think that the music industry is filled with people who are just as passionate about music as I am. Not so. No one, and I mean NO ONE, is as passionate about my music as me. There definitely are people in music for the right reasons, but there are just as many who have gotten jaded and lost their way. Some of the good ones gave up too early when success was just around the corner. Team members, publicists, band mates, managers, and labels…they all come and go. The music industry isn't a charity or a church—if the money disappears then eventually the people do, too. That new belief about the people I was working with has helped me immensely. My advice is, be on guard, don't give control over your work, money, or career to just anybody. And that goes for anybody, in any industry.

My hero, Peter Daniels, an Australian businessman, author, and speaker, once asked a question that I like to ask myself sometimes: Do I really have what it takes? Can I get the job done? Truthfully, the answer changes day to day. Most mornings I leap out of bed ready to take on the world, and other times I feel like doing nothing. I think the answer lies in the condition of my mind, in my thoughts. In the blink of an eye, I can realize I'm thinking negatively, and stop the cycle of negative thinking. This changes my mood completely and puts a smile on my face. Everyone can see it: my wife, my friends, my band members. And now my whole outlook for the day is altered.

The point I'm trying to make is that we have to choose what we think—or what we think will choose for us.

"Get control of your thoughts and you'll get control of your life." —Manafest

GREAT WALL OF CHINA

IN THE STUDIO WITH SETH MOSLEY IN NASHVILLE, TN

WRITING NEW MUSIC

LIVE ALBUM STAGE

PHOTO SHOOT IN HOLLYWOOD, CA

not about how you [start?]
but how you finish.
John 16:33
10:10
[invest] in people things
not things
WHAT WOULD YOU DO IF YOU KNEW
you could NOT FAIL
the things to Love People
919!!
SELF PUBLISH?
or
Book Deal?
Fighter
I never said I wouldn't break down

Courage!!
Perseverance
Mindset
DISCIPLINE
Will Power
Poser!!
What do you really want??
The five keys to conquering fear
and reaching your dreams
JOURNAL
What will you trade your life for? first law of success is to maintain control
2013

Fighter Book
where
Dreams
become
reality
If God is for me
whom shall I fear
Psalms 18:37
If You for me
who could be
against me
I don't need
a Book Deal

$LIVE TO GIVE$
if we do not get
then we cannot give
and the enemy has won
JESUS IS LORD
NO MORE!!
Isaiah 54:17
thoughts become words
words become actions
Perfect love casts out fear
actions become habits
habits shows character
where strength finds purpose
Character becomes
Destiny
Leadership is Loneliness
quit
First Century
S O S

Sister
mom
Canada
USO
Australia
Japan
Melanie
DREAMS dream big
VISIONS
write it down
GOALS
time frames measurements
Skating
music
Performing
writing
teaching
healing
Failure is
not an option
Words have power
SLAVE TO THE
call Shannon
Skype Interview
NO PLAN B PUSHOVER
Romans 12:12
Must Release by spring 2013
Love never fails because God is
love & God never fails
looking to give not get
STOP company myself
to offer people

Write not just
for me but what
it does for others
My Journey
My Struggle
Victory
TO THE
Forget the
LENDER
Build in Recovery

ACTION STEPS:

1) The first thing that used to come to mind in response to stress is "I can't do it." I turned this phrase around and put a positive spin on it so now when I'm stressed out I say "I can do all things through Christ who strengthens me." Now it's your turn; identify three negative phrases your mind comes up with in response to stress. Now write down three positive affirmations to counteract each one.

Negative phrase:

Positive affirmation:

Negative phrase:

Positive affirmation:

Negative phrase:

Positive affirmation:

2) I have what I call an inspirational journal. Start one for yourself, and dedicate a few minutes every day to writing one page of inspirational phrases, quotes, lyrics, or other positive messages.

MIND MASTER PRAYER

LORD CLEANSE MY HEART
CLEANSE MY MIND
CAST AWAY ALL THOSE THOUGHTS THAT BIND
SO I CAN LET YOUR LIGHT SHINE
LET YOUR WILL BE MINE
I WANNA SEE DIVINE
AS I SEEK TO FIND
LET ME SEE THE SIGN
IN TIME THE DAY UNWINDS
LET YOUR FIRE REFINE
I RHYME AND LEAVE THIS WORLD BEHIND
BEING KIND WITH A LOVE THAT'S BLIND
NO CASTING PEARLS TO THE SWINE
BE THE MASTER OF MY MIND
AND LET YOUR SPIRIT REMIND
INCLINE MY EAR TO HEAR
I WAS BLIND
NOW I SEE CLEAR WITH FEAR
WILL YOU APPEAR TO A MERE MAN?
HELP ME UNDERSTAND YOUR WAY
I'M PRAYING DAY TO DAY
YOU CAN BE MY POTTER
I WILL BE YOUR CLAY
LET ME LIVE FOR YOU TODAY
THIS IS WHAT I PRAY LORD
THIS IS WHAT I PRAY

-CHRIS WATT

Discipline

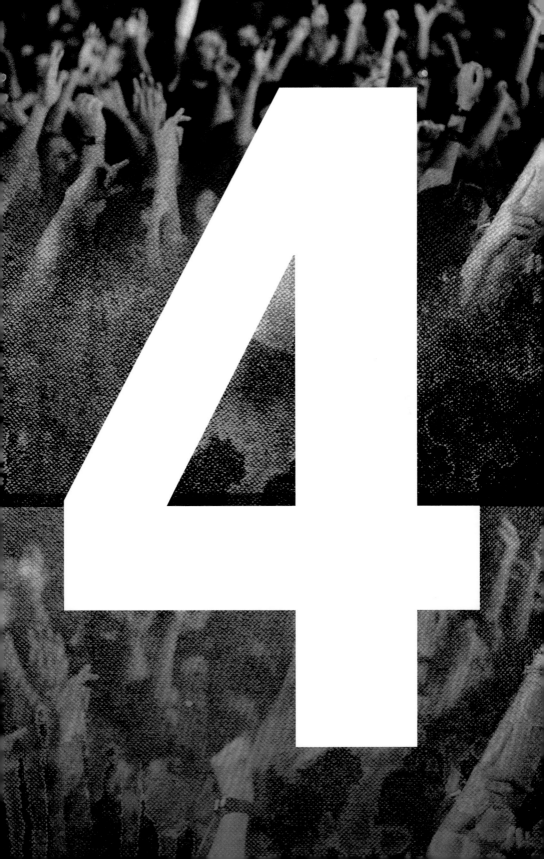

Chapter Four
DISCIPLINE

I could have been hanging out with Lady Gaga; instead, I was in my hotel room, resting for the next day. I can't tell you how many nights I've spent gazing at some gorgeous skyline from the window of a hotel room in a city I couldn't go play in. That night I was in Osaka, Japan, with my band, for the second time. We finished playing our show, signed autographs, and everyone got cleaned up to go out to eat. Osaka has to be one of the most inspiring cities for fashion and art, not to mention it has one of the coolest outdoor skate parks in the world. I wanted to hang out all night, but I knew I had interviews early in the morning, and I'd be useless unless I got some sleep.

The next day I had to listen to the guys bragging about what a great time they had, seeing Lady Gaga and meeting her band. She happened to be playing in Osaka the same night we did—talk about a small world! It's sacrifices like these that hurt, but discipline always pays off, eventually. When you make decisions to discipline your mind and body and adhere to them, it flushes out fear, and replaces it with faith. I once heard Ronnie Faisst, a bronze medal champ of the X Games for motocross give his testimony while working his butt off at home training. He said, "The X Games are won here." He meant the crazy steep hill he would run up every day, or doing relentless pushups, or going around the racetrack again and again, building up his muscle memory by doing stunts. He meant that discipline was how he won his medals. Discipline prepared him for what the future would bring.

I use discipline to hone my craft as a performer, and as a writer.

In the early days of developing my talents as an artist, I remember spending New Year's Eve, among other nights, alone. I'd sit in my basement and practice writing songs, then perform them in front of the mirror to sharpen my skills. I'm naturally an introvert, so I was used to being alone, but it wasn't always easy when I knew my friends were out having fun. I used discipline to push through writer's block. I'd fill up my wastepaper basket over and over with crumpled pieces of paper. I'd stand up and pace back and forth for hours just to get one line, or sometimes nothing at all. I thought it wasn't working, but little did I know that this discipline was building the foundation that I am now standing on.

Discipline is a skill; we're not born with it. You have to learn how to say no, because it's almost always easier to say yes. Here are some of my favorite examples of a disciplined life. In other words, this is what I was actually doing all those years, instead of doing whatever I felt like doing or whatever others wanted me to do.

"Eating ice cream is easy, making something that matters is hard." —Seth Godin

RADIO TKO

"Effort only fully releases its reward after a person refuses to quit." — Napoleon Hill

I've gotten so many rejection emails from record labels, managers, and booking agents, I could print them out and fill this book with them, or wallpaper every room in my house. Well, maybe not that many—but, dang, there's been a lot! The whole point of getting a manager, in my opinion, is to have someone who can help you form relationships with people who can leverage your career. Managers can help you get onto bigger tours, opening for better bands, and get you sponsorships, festivals, and songwriting collaborations. The list can go on and on, but the point is, with proper management and good songs, an artist can take off fast.

The typical response you get from any music manager when you're being rejected is, "Our roster is full right now and we're focusing on the artists we currently have, but check back with us in six months." I'd dutifully follow up with them only to find out they just signed one of my friend's bands. Are you kidding me? That's the unfortunate thing about the music business; truth be told, it's who you know. One manager, I reached out to for about three years. He was really nice about turning me down. He even invited me to meet with him at his office and gave me a bunch of advice. He seemed bummed he couldn't help me out more, and said he always thought I should be bigger. It was a great pat on the back, but nothing came of it.

I didn't let it stop me. I kept pursuing my dreams, touring, writing songs, and releasing records without a manager. Eventually I got a radio hit. One of the radio promoters kept bugging the president of Tooth & Nail Records, saying, "'Avalanche' is a hit. It's a hit!" My song "Avalanche" continued to climb the charts, and I got massive exposure, which helped hugely with touring, and put my music in front of people who had never heard of me. Record sales tripled for The Chase, and increased the merchandise sales at my online store. At its peak, "Avalanche" hit number four on the Christian Contemporary Hit Radio charts and made an appearance in Billboard magazine. I was stoked! I took a picture of it and sent it to my wife right away.

My phone started ringing, and offers started coming in from bands and their managers for me to tour with them. I remember I was on tour at the time, and I had just gotten off the stage when I got a call from the manager I mentioned earlier. He said he'd heard a lot of great things, and that my songs were playing nonstop on the radio. Now, all of a sudden, he was interested in working with me! For three years I tried to work with this guy, and nothing ever came of it, until I finally got through. Radio opened the doors I couldn't have opened myself just touring; it allowed me to be in a thousand places at once. (Let me also say there are many bands that have done it without radio—so if you're not a radio-friendly band, don't worry.)

Radio was a hard nut to crack, and I'd like to share another story about that, because it didn't happen overnight, and I put a lot of work into it.

"Discipline is the bridge between goals and accomplishment." —Jim Rohn

I hired two companies to do radio promotions for me in Canada, and both were professional and hardworking, but they couldn't produce results. They always returned my phone calls, and gave me detailed reports, but still no radio ads for Manafest! Efforts don't pay the bills, results do. As you can imagine, this got expensive, quickly. It was frustrating, because the company I really wanted to hire wouldn't call me back or respond to my emails. In the music industry, the real professionals don't just work with anyone. They can afford to be picky, and only work with the artists they truly believe have a hit song. That way, the radio stations trust that what they bring them is quality material. If they started lowering their standards for a quick buck, it would hurt their business in the long run. On the other hand, there are some people in the industry who claim to be pros, and talk a good game. They tell you just what you want to hear, and they're happy to take your money whether or not your song does well, because they have their own bills to pay. So, be cautious.

How did I crack radio in Canada? I disciplined myself to make time every couple of weeks, and sent the radio team I wanted to work with short emails, keeping them up to date on what was happening with my career—without being too annoying, of course. I was starting to have some success, so I sent a polite reminder highlighting my latest achievements, and that's how "the squeaky wheel got the grease."

Here is an example of the email I would send:

Hey Guys,

Hope you are well.

I just wanted to keep you updated with what's going on:

I was recently nominated for a second JUNO Award. We just finished a North American tour, playing for 500–1,000 people a night, and now I'm back home. I've currently sold over 3,000 copies of my album, The Chase, in Canada, and I'd love it if you guys would consider working one of my singles to radio.

Here's a link to my latest music video and songs: http://www.manafest.net

Thanks again, and I look forward to hearing from you.

Chris

After numerous emails and phone calls, one day my phone buzzed. It was a response from a radio promoter! Finally. We set up a phone meeting to chat about the songs, and it turned out that one of the owners of the company grew up in the Durham area, in the same town I did. It was an instant connection. Finding common ground can make a big difference. He said they listened to the record, and they thought my song "Every Time You Run" could work for Hot AC Radio. The gloves started coming off! I wanted to smash this radio door open!

"First," he said, "You have to make some edits to the song so it fits the Hot AC Radio format that stations are looking for." Some artists get bent out of shape when they're told to change their music, but I wasn't about to bang down this guy's door asking for help and then not listen to what he had to say. So I said, "Whatever you need, man, consider it done." We sped up the tempo of "Every Time You Run" and added a snippet of the chorus to play at the very beginning. Not a big deal. But even then, after nailing all their changes, they still gave me a big disclaimer. It's not that they were hesitant or didn't think the song was any good, but they just wanted to be clear—they would do everything they could, but couldn't guarantee the radio stations would add my song. That sounded strange, because all the other promoters I'd worked with before were optimistic. Then again, they also made promises they couldn't keep.

So, here we go again; another radio campaign. Except this time it was going to cost me just over $8,000 to promote my song for three or four months, and even longer if it started to do well.

After the first week of promo, radio stations began adding the single. One of the first stations was CHUM FM—this was huge! And MuchMusic added my music video into heavy rotation. I flipped out when I heard this! (If this happened today in California, I'd do a victory lap around our house on my skateboard.) This meant that "Every Time You Run" would play on one of the biggest radio stations in Toronto, including in my hometown of Pickering. Friends I hadn't heard from since public school and family members started contacting me on Facebook to congratulate me. I felt like a hometown hero with my first commercial radio hit in Canada. It was a crazy time, and I loved every second of it. I was nominated for artist of the month by a radio network with multiple stations across the country, and all at once, thousands of people across Canada were listening to my song.

Even though "Every Time You Run" was doing well in Canada, it wasn't connecting with radio stations right away in the United States. We heard all kinds of excuses: "There's too much rap in the song." Or, "If it sounded more like TobyMac, we'd add it."

My wife and I prayed, asking God that radio stations would see the vision of the song. The record label was behind me, and I truly believed this song could impact lives—so we mobilized my fans to start requesting the song at radio stations in the United States. Weeks later, one of the stations did some testing and came back with positive results. We took these results to other stations as proof, and one by one, stations began playing the song. "Every Time You Run" resonated with the listeners, and ended up in the top ten charts. Best of all, I've heard countless stories from fans about how the song touched their lives and continues to do so. When I was in Texas recently, a woman told me she was praying for her son to give his life back to God, but he wasn't interested. I always share my story about how God set me free from fear and my childhood struggles before I sing "Every Time You Run." For the first time, her son bought something Christian—my CD. He told her, "Mom, what he said tonight, and that song, got through to me." She thanked me with tears in her eyes, hugged me, and walked away.

That's a TKO!

GOOD ISN'T GOOD ENOUGH

"What a person does on a disciplined, consistent basis gets him ready no matter what the goal."— John Maxwell

One of the most common questions I get from young artists is, "How do I get signed?" It's important to note that signing a record deal isn't the final victory lap in your music career, with you running through the red ribbon saying, "I've made it!" Signing a deal is just one of the many small steps towards building a successful career in the music industry.

Let me say it right now that you don't need a record label to get started on a music career. You can write and record something in your home studio, and for less than sixty bucks, have it distributed online through TuneCore or CDBaby. These services can make your music available almost worldwide on iTunes, Amazon, Spotify, and many other digital platforms. It's not like it used to be when record labels were the gatekeepers that only let a select chosen few through the door. Plus, it's all about online sales these days. Don't go after brick-and-mortar stores; they're dying out.

Even if you do sign with a label, you're the one touring and peddling your CD across the globe, not them. You're going to be the most passionate about your music, not anyone else, and never forget that. Just recently, I've worked with about seven different record labels around the world—in India, the United States, Canada, Europe, South Africa, and Japan. However, these aren't all official record deals, but what is called a licensing deal, in which I still retain ownership of the masters. My recommendation to any artist is to stay independent as long as you can until you need a label to do what you can't do yourself. The truth is, you can do more and get paid more as an independent artist than you think. You just have to try!

The key to my success in signing with a record label was consistency. And being consistent takes discipline. At first, the record labels didn't like my music because I still needed time to develop; it wasn't good enough. Good isn't good enough. There are lots of musicians out there making music that we all agree is good.

But how much of it is great?

Most of the people I know who work at record labels are very passionate about music, and they could probably make more money doing something else, but because of their passion for music and its ability to touch people's lives, they stay in the game. But if they want to keep their jobs, they have to produce best-selling records. Before a label signs any artist, the higher-ups of the label first ask, "Can we make money off this artist? Will it sell?" If not, unfortunately, they will pass. There used to be a day when A&R reps of record labels had more signing authority to take risks on bands. Now, because budgets are so tight with many labels going out of business, they could lose their jobs if they sign one wrong act!

DESTINY IS NEVER LATE

"I will study and prepare, and someday my opportunity will come." —Abraham Lincoln

I've come to learn it's never been about me sitting around waiting for someone to open the door; I've always had to kick the door down. I never sit on the sidelines waiting for God to show up. I like to get in there and get my hands dirty anticipating a breakthrough. I may not get the answers I want at the time I want them, but let me tell you that no matter how long it takes or how many chances you need to get it right—destiny is never late.

Trevor McNevan from the band Thousand Foot Krutch had an intricate role in my success as an artist. I originally met the Canadian singer in Hamilton, Ontario, at their CD release party for the album Set it Off. I'll never forget the stage we played on there, because the audience could walk around the whole thing in a circle. I opened for them two nights in a row with a few other bands, and Trevor and I hit it off immediately; afterwards, we kept in touch. Whenever they played locally or shot a music video, Melanie and I would drive across town to support them. We were fans of their music back then, and still are.

I was still working at my office job when I got a call from Trevor one day. He said I was on his heart, and he wanted to help me with my music career. He invited me over to play him some of the music I'd recorded, and he shared some of the tunes he was working on as well. He said they'd recently got out of a deal and were now signing with Tooth & Nail Records. He told me about the music business, managers, booking agents, and told me stories about touring. I got super excited because Trevor genuinely wanted to help me out. I've had other artists offer to help me, but there was always a long, sketchy contract sitting at the end of the table. This time there were no strings attached. Within two months, Trevor set up a showcase for me to play for the president of Tooth & Nail Records at a venue called the Market Hall in Peterborough, Ontario.

I don't know about you, but when a close friend recommends a restaurant, or a movie, or a new band, I normally take it to heart and give it a chance. That's exactly how I got introduced to a label for the first time. Because Trevor was the one recommending me, the president listened to my songs with more of an open mind. If I had just sent my music to him myself, he might have listened, but it wouldn't have had the same chance. It's all about the introduction, and whom it comes from, in the music business. There are so many gatekeepers; you have to get passed all the naysayers. Even if you convince one person at a label, that person now has to get the rest of the office behind it.

I was so stoked about the showcase that my DJ and I practiced every night for almost two weeks straight. We wanted our show planned out perfectly, down to the last second. I also find that the more prepared you are, the easier it is to switch it up on the fly if something goes wrong. We rehearsed in his basement until 1 a.m. most nights, going through the intro, the songs, and what I'd say in between. I still had to wake up early for work, though, and one night we were up so late, that I fell asleep during a meeting the next day. My boss and I were visiting another company that we were thinking of hiring for our systems, and it was so boring I began to nod off. When we got in the car afterward to drive back to the office, my boss gave me an earful. He told me it was embarrassing that I nodded off, and to just stay home next time I'm going to be in that condition. I felt pretty whack about it, and I never let it happen again.

The day of the showcase came fast, and I invited all of my friends to help me pack the place. This was the night I was getting signed! We arrived early at the venue to set up the merchandise and do a sound check, and it was the first time I got to meet the Hawk Nelson guys. I had the merchandise table looking pro with my laptop playing my music video for the song "Session," and I had just finished setting up, when I bumped into the president of Tooth & Nail Records. I was surprised at how down-to-earth he was. We talked about touring, music, and skateboarding; he wasn't anything like I'd pictured the president of a record label would be. He came across as just another fan of music and very genuine. Now I was even more excited to play.

By the time the show started, the place was packed with some rowdy kids. We played a crazy live performance, got the audience involved, and rocked their faces off. In a flash, our set was done and the curtains closed. During the set change, Daniel Biro from Hawk Nelson said, "Go get that record deal, bro. You guys killed it!" When I got offstage, Trevor and the president of Tooth & Nail said they loved my set. My friends gave me daps and pounds, and I was smiling ear to ear. The night couldn't have gone better—until it all took a nosedive.

One of my producers at the time kept urging me to have the meeting that night with the president and seal the deal. He kept saying, "Don't exclude us now, bro." So I asked Trevor if we could meet about the record deal briefly, and he agreed. We all sat down with the president of the label. The problem was that it wasn't just my producer in the room; a few of my crew came in, too.

Immediately my friend started shooting off his mouth. "How much is the advance going to be? Do we get a budget for a music video? What about marketing—what is the label going to do?" It was absolutely the wrong way to start a record deal meeting. I hadn't even been given a formal offer yet—it wasn't the time for negotiations! I was totally embarrassed. I started kicking him under the table with my foot, but he wouldn't shut up. The president of the label looked a little ticked off, and the meeting ended quickly. But I said good-bye to him and Trevor and I drove home that night thinking everything would be OK.

The moral of the story obviously is: Never bring your hip-hop crew to a business meeting. Sure enough, right after lunch the next day, my cell phone rang. It was Trevor. I shut the door to my office immediately, thinking, Sweet! He's going to tell me what Tooth & Nail thought about the show and talk about the deal.

Instead he told me he felt like I had broken his trust because of what took place in the meeting, and he couldn't help me anymore. My heart dropped to the floor. I started crying on the phone and tried to apologize for what happened. Trevor was upset, too, but he had to follow his heart; he wished me all the best and hung up the phone. We parted ways.

I was devastated. I couldn't tell if I was more angry, or hurt, or what—there were so many emotions running through my mind that day. Here I had a great job that I was successful at; I didn't need music to earn a living. A few times while I was driving home that day I thought, That's it. I'm done, forget it. I was up; I was down. I was swearing, crying, and punching my steering wheel. I parked on the side of the road around the corner from Melanie's house, and sat there screaming and bawling my eyes out.

In the midst of the panic and disappointment, somehow the original dream God gave me surfaced in my mind. It was an image of me performing in front of a sea of people and sharing Jesus. It reminded me that it wasn't just about the music; there was a message God wanted me to deliver. I felt God gave me an assignment, and until I'd completed it, I wasn't done. I wanted to quit so badly. I was tired of pushing and pulling, trying to make it happen on my own. I felt like a rat in its wheel, running, running, and getting nowhere. Maybe that was the problem: all this time I was trying to make it happen on my own, instead of letting God do His thing.

I knew I had to keep going, and discipline was what got me through. I kept writing, performing, and kept a healthier balance with life, church, and work. I finished recording the appropriately named album My Own Thing and released it in Canada. About a year after it was out, I called Trevor just to keep him in the loop, and I was shocked that he still wanted to help me. (Of course, only if my friends or producers weren't involved in any way.)

I recorded more music, and released the hit song "Skills" featuring Trevor from Thousand Foot Krutch, and I did eventually sign with Tooth & Nail Records, who released my first international album Epiphany in 2006. It was such a long road of twists and turns, bumps, and potholes—but because my discipline had prepared me I made it. I can still see myself standing in my sunroom in my condo on a sunny afternoon when the president phoned me. He said, "Manafest, I want to license your records and do a three-album deal with you.

These are the points and terms. Cool?" I was like, "OK, draft it up." He said, "Our lawyer will send you a deal memo shortly," and that was it. I hung up the phone and did circles around my tiny condo with my wife! This was the beginning of something great, and I felt like David killing Goliath! Little did I know the journey had just begun.

"The discipline you learn and the character you build from setting and achieving a goal can be more valuable than achievement of the goal itself." —Bo Bennett

MANAFEST

FIGHTER

CANADA TOUR

IN THE RING

JAN. 9 / RED DEER, AB   JAN. 14 / WETASKIWIN, AB
JAN. 10 / KAMLOOPS, BC   JAN. 18 / LETHBRIDGE, AB
JAN. 11 / DIDSBURY, AB   JAN. 19 / MOOSE JAW, SK
JAN. 12 / YORKTON, SK   JAN. 20 / REGINA, SK
JAN 13 / SASKATOON, SK

MANAFEST.NET

Welcome to HOLLYWOOD

6906½

WRITING WITH TREVOR MCNEVAN AND ADAM MESSINGER

FILMING "EVERY TIME YOUR RUN" VIDEO IN HAMILTON, ONTARIO

LIVE RADIO INTERVIEW IN OSAKA, JAPAN

IN STORE EVENT IN TOKYO

ナダの一人LINKIN PARK

MANAFEST

新作をひっさげ
激ロック出演のため来日!!

NEW ALBUM!!
『The Chas
2010.2.3 ON S

/12(Fri)@新宿MARZ

t's up Japan and all you Geki-Rockers!
you in February !!
はどうだい!？日本のみんなと激ロッカーたち!
に会おうぜ！」(from MANAFEST)

ミクスチャー 一匹狼の真剣勝負!!

MANAFEST

ACTION STEPS:

1). Make a list of three things you can do daily that require discipline. Job-hunting? Journaling? Making time for your family? Then set reminders in your phone to do them.

2) Make a list of three things you do daily that lack discipline. Watching TV? Complaining? Oversleeping?

Willpower

Chapter Five
WILLPOWER

Give it just a little bit more.
A fighter isn't someone who never fails.
A fighter is someone who never quits.

Have you ever tried opening a jar that's so tight you can't budge it? You grab a butter knife, pound the lid against the countertop, use a kitchen towel to get a better grip—but no matter what you do, the stupid thing won't open. Finally, you're standing there, twisting and twisting, hands sore, face wrinkling with the strain, and just when you're about to give up, you hear a pop. The lid comes off. That's WILLPOWER.

Willpower is an internal force that pushes you to give it just a little bit more. Your end goal may only be to get some jam or some tasty pickles out of a jar, but the point is, you had a goal in mind for your will to act upon. What does it mean when someone has a strong will to win? It means they want it bad enough. They're not easily shaken from their goal.

Sometimes that last little push is the difference between success and failure. Willpower is the internal part of you that moves you to action. Willpower is the opposite of doing whatever you want, whenever you want. Willpower will make you stand, when you want to drop to your knees.

Whenever I need a burst of energy to make a decision or act immediately, I draw on my will. Some mornings, I'm exhausted, and my alarm is going off, and I know I should get up, but I don't. Then all of a sudden, I jump out of bed, running, focused, and on a mission to get something done today.

Other times, I've caught myself sitting around waiting for someone to email me and rescue me, put me inside my dreams. Willpower doesn't take life as it comes. It grabs life with both hands and squeezes everything you can out of it.

"Life doesn't hand you your dreams." —Dave Ramsey

I look at all the decisions I've made over the years and the circumstances I've been exposed to. I don't believe I just ended up here by chance; I have an amazing gift called "the power of choice." I've thought about it many times: What would my life look like if my father hadn't committed suicide? If I didn't get hurt skateboarding, would I still have started a music career? Would I still be working in IT if I hadn't quit my job? If I hadn't pursued Melanie, would we have still gotten married?

The choices I made, I willed myself to make them. They were my decisions, no finger-pointing or excuses. I'm here today because of the paths I chose to take yesterday.

Willpower and choice are connected.

How many times have I seen this in my life? From the food I eat, to my exercise program, to my goal-setting exercises, to how I manage money and my relationships. Sometimes I don't "will" myself to do anything, because I don't know what I really want.

Willpower is a fighter's tool. Make the correct choices, forget your past, live strong in the present, and dream of your future. This is my definition of willpower.

THIS IS A TEST

"A man will do things when he's drunk that he'd never do when he's sober." —Kenneth Copeland

There's a reason why I don't go out after shows: there are usually a lot of girls around.

I don't like putting myself in compromising positions. I'm not perfect, and I'm not looking to see how close I can get to the edge without falling off. I feel like this is a test of two wills—my flesh and my spirit.

I once heard about a man, mid forties, married, successful, with two beautiful children, who was found crying in a church pew with his hands over his face. He'd thrown away his marriage, sacrificed his dreams for the future, damaged his character, and lost his kid's respect—and he couldn't even remember the girl's name.

It's a heart-wrenching story, and I promised myself I'd never follow in those footsteps. In my industry, promiscuous sex and drug use are rampant. The older I get, the more tragedies I witness.

I was on a club tour across the west coast of Canada one time, opening for a larger act. It was just Melanie and me for the first two weeks. We were the only Christians on the tour, and we didn't say much about our faith to the others, except for when they shared their personal hardships with us. I think what impacted them the most was the way Melanie and I were with each other. We were in love, and it was real. I wasn't cheating on Melanie; we weren't out getting drunk or doing drugs. We watched the guys fighting with their girlfriends on their cell phones, cheating on them every opportunity that presented it self.

The rock 'n' roll lifestyle—sleeping around with a bunch of girls—is such a lie. It promises fame, fortune, and a great time, but all it delivers is pain.

Of course, the first night my wife was gone, two blonde girls approached me after my show. My tour manager was chatting them up while we were hanging out. I politely said hello to the girls, then excused myself. As I'm packing up my merchandise, the girls came up to me again, and asked me what I was doing later. They said, "We were told to follow you back to your hotel." I laughed, because on this tour I didn't get a hotel room. I was planning on asking the guys if I could sleep on the floor of their room. I told them, "Sorry, you'll have to talk to the other guys."

It doesn't sound like much of a test of will, like it was an easy decision. And it was. Because my will is connected to certain principles and values; it's like a guiding light clinging to my feet, that guides me to making a decision without hesitation. If I didn't know where I stood on the issues of faithfulness and integrity, then maybe I would have been swayed.

It's hard to make decisions when you're double-minded. James 1:8 says, "a double-minded man is unstable in all his ways."

But the story doesn't end here, so keep reading.

So, I end up in one of the hotel rooms with some of the guys from the show. I was hanging out, listening to tunes on my computer, sprawled out on the bed. The drinks started flowing, smoke filled the room, and of course the two girls walked in. I was like, "Oh no." I got up and walked to the other guy's hotel room to get away from the craziness. I asked if I could sleep in their room instead. They said yes, so I went back to the other room where everyone was partying to get my laptop. By some weird coincidence, I opened the door to the room and instead of music I heard the voice of Mark Barclay, a hardcore preacher from Michigan, playing from my laptop. I was stunned. I circled the room with my eyes; nobody had noticed that sermon of hellfire and damnation blasting in the background.

I finished that tour without sacrificing my character, my marriage, or what I truly believed in. I also made some new friends. There were dozens of times my will was tested, but I remember that man who gave up his lifetime of happiness for fifteen minutes of pleasure.

Willpower enables you to make decisions now that you won't regret later on.

GIVE IT JUST A LITTLE BIT MORE

One night in 2006 after a show I drove all the way from Cheyenne, Wyoming, to Rialto, California, in my Pontiac minivan. It's a pretty dull drive most of the way, except for the mountains in Salt Lake City. At midnight I crossed into Nevada, and I was excited to see the Vegas lights ahead. It was my first time seeing the famous gamblers' city. I was amazed at all the crazy hotels; a giant black pyramid; MGM's lions; and casino lights everywhere that lit up the sky. I was so enthralled by the spectacle that I rolled all the way through Vegas and 30-plus minutes past before I noticed my gas light was on.

I freaked out. I'd been so busy looking out my window I forgot to fill up on gas, and now it was 2 a.m. and I was somewhere out in the middle of the desert. I called myself an idiot. I started saying my prayers, hugged the steering wheel, and tried not to think about every scary movie I'd ever seen. What if I got stuck out here with no cell phone reception? There was hardly another vehicle on the road; I was alone.

After what seemed like an eternity, I saw a gleaming object on the horizon—a gas station! I never thought I'd be so happy to see a gas station in my life. I still remember smiling ear to ear and dancing around while pumping my gas. The cashier must have thought I was on drugs.

I crossed the California state line around 3 a.m., absolutely exhausted. All the hotels were booked, or too expensive. I felt powerless. I had no money, no energy, and nowhere to sleep.

I rolled the window down and spit on the pavement outside the door of the van after brushing my teeth using bottled water. I ended up sleeping in my van that night in the Walmart parking lot. Falling asleep was easy because I was so tired, but I kept waking up, startled by different noises outside the van, thinking someone might be trying to break in.

That morning I woke up to California sunshine and city noises, and a breakfast served to me through the drive-through window of McDonald's. Nobody knew the kind of night I'd had, and I still had to show up at the venue the next day with a smile on my face, ready to rock the house.

The comfort of my own bed and my wife at home lingered in my head. My will was up against some strong opposition. Should I just forget this crap, the financial stress, the fears and insecurities, and go back to my home and my comfy office job?

Willpower is the quality in people that separates the mediocre from the great.

I kept going.

Why? It wasn't the money; I was hardly getting paid. It wasn't the fame; I barely had fans back then. There must be a sense of purpose behind what I was doing; otherwise I would have turned right around and gone back home. I remembered a moment in my life where God spoke to me and gave me a vision of performing in front of a sea of people, changing lives, and sharing the message of love through my music. That was my motivation, and I was "willing" to do it at any cost.

HELL WEEK

I like reading about the vigorous training Navy SEALS do—it strengthens my willpower. At the height of their training, some of the classes of trainees only get two to five hours of sleep with continuous drills simulating warfare and tests of endurance. It's called Hell Week. They're woken up at some ungodly hour by the sound of gunfire, with live rounds, going off—a sound much louder than blanks. The men are led into chest-deep freezing ocean water, shivering, waiting for the whistle to blow, and then they charge back up onto the beach, crawling on their bellies with only the friction of the sand against their bodies to warm them just past the edge of hypothermia. Then, it's back in the water again.

At the height of the week, to taunt the men, the sergeants make comments like, "If you quit now, we got fresh coffee and donuts for you. Just let us know."

Whether they stand there with teeth chattering on the shore, or grit their teeth in courage, there is one common quality between all the men who survive Hell Week. These men have the ability to step outside of themselves, endure the pain, and focus on how they can help the man standing next to them. It's not about being a hero—it's about laying down your life for your teammates, pulling each other up, pushing forward, and leaving no one behind.

I wasn't the most talented musician when I started rapping and writing music. In fact, I was probably the least talented. Even now it takes a team of people to develop the songs I write and polish them for release. These are the people I'm so grateful for, like my wife and friends, who believe in me even when I don't believe in myself.

Maybe you're going through something right now that feels like the toughest fight of your life. You might think you're at your breaking point. Imagine it's Hell Week and you're in training. Don't quit now because the greatest breakthrough of your life is just around the corner. Can I encourage you? Can I pull you up, and push you forward, like a soldier standing by your side?

POWER TO CHOOSE

Willpower is power because it gives you a choice. Most people in life don't think they have a choice. They think they are thrown into circumstances, that the reactions they get from others are arbitrary, or they think they are victims, and live life at the whims of circumstance. When you realize that this is false, and that you do have a choice, you have power.

There's a Bible story that illustrates willpower well. It's the story of Shadrach, Meshach, and Abednego. These three men stood strong on their faith when their lives were in danger. Nebuchadnezzar the king, wanted them to worship him. They had a choice. He told them to bow down, but they would not.

Nebuchadnezzar threatened them with death, and their bodies would be thrown into the fire, but they didn't change their stance. They would not bow down. The king, true to his word, had the three men thrown into the fire. God met them in the fire, appearing as a fourth man walking around, and not a single flame damaged their clothes or skin.

Shadrach, Meshach, and Abednego didn't know whether God was going to show up or not. But they knew that they couldn't bow down. When I'm faced with tough decisions, especially when it comes to morals and integrity, I remember that I always have a choice. And the principles and values I have put in place guide my will.

The mixture of willpower, strong beliefs, and principles makes you an individual that is not easily shaken. Some people think of willpower as self-control, a force that holds them back from doing something. That's close, but not entirely correct. Willpower is the self-directed energy behind self-control. Willpower doesn't hold you back; it pushes you forward, allowing you to do something great.

You were born during this time, in this country, to do something great while you're here living on this earth. There are no accidental humans. We all have a purpose for our life. The question is, now that you know you're born to do something great, what will you do? Whatever it is, big or small, you only have one lifetime to do it in—so you better start today!

"Will Power is essential to the accomplishment of anything worthwhile." —Brian Tracy

ORIGINAL "FIRE IN THE KITCHEN" MASKS

PERFORMING IN OSAKA, JAPAN

"RENEGADE" VIDEO SHOOT IN HAMILTON, ONTARIO

"FIRE IN THE KITCHEN" VIDEO SHOOT IN HAMILTON, ONTARIO

LIVE IN CONCERT

"NEVER LET YOU GO" VIDEO SHOOT IN CANNES, FRANCE

ACTION STEPS:

1. Sharing God's message through my music is what engages my willpower when I need it most. What motivates you to go the extra distance?

2. Write down two times you've used your willpower to stick something out. Finishing your homework? Staying late to finish a project at work? Another 15 minutes in the gym? Choosing to forgive someone who wronged you again?

"I WAS BO
BUT CHOS
MAN. WHE
A MAN. I A
A FIGHTER;
I BECAME A
STARTED T
MY DESTIN

RN A MALE,
F TO BE A'
I I BECAME
SO BECAME
AND WHEN
FIGHTER. I
WALK IN
Y". MANAFEST

Chapter Six
KNOCK OUT

Now that you understand the five keys to being a fighter, I can talk about some of the other concepts that fuel the fight against our fears.

Remember that scene from the movie Walk the Line when Johnny Cash auditions for an opportunity to get his band signed with Sun Records? They sang some old-school track by Jimmie Davis, and it sounded good, but there was something missing. It didn't come across as believable. Sam Phillips, the owner of the label and the one auditioning the group, interrupted Johnny midway through the song and asked him, "Have you got anything else?" Of course, Cash gets offended (like most artists do when their music is being criticized), but it appears he also wants to understand, so he can improve. Phillips continues to challenge him, saying, "If you was hit by a truck and you was lying out there in that gutter dying, and you had time to sing one song, huh? One song that people would remember before you're dirt; one song that would let God know how you felt about your time here on earth; one song that would sum you up—you're telling me that's the song you'd sing?"

Johnny Cash replies, "I wrote some songs while I was in the air force," and ends up singing about his experiences at war, with a tune that would become his hit song "Folsom Prison Blues." That was a song that came right from his heart, it was believable, and millions of people connected with it. That's the key to writing great music; it has to come from the heart.

You would think that using our hearts would make us weaker, not stronger, but like the movie version of Cash's experience, it's the reverse that happens. If you want to connect with people, you have to make yourself vulnerable. For me, coming from the heart and being a fighter are deeply connected.

It's not strange to talk about the two in the same sentence: Boxers and other fighters are referred to as having "a lot of heart," all the time. Having heart doesn't mean that you're the best fighter; or that you'll never face adversity; or that you can't fail; or get knocked out; or never feel fear—it means that you care deeply about the fight. Win or lose, you're giving it your all.

It has always been my goal to touch millions of people with my music. There came a moment in my career when I decided that I cared. I let my life do the talking, my heart do the guiding, and used music as the platform to share my stories and beliefs. My fans are grateful, and I've never regretted it.

Here's another one of our cultural heroes who gave it his all.

WHO'S YOUR MICKEY?

Rocky. Think of Sylvester Stallone getting knocked around the ring like a rag doll. His legs are shaking like jelly, barely holding him up, and he stares at his opponent with two swollen eyes; it looks like the fight is over. The referee is about to call it. Rocky turns to his coach, Mickey, and says, "I can't go another round. I can't do it." Mickey shouts, "Get up and go one more round!" Those words inspire Rocky to find the inner strength to bounce back up, and with more tenacity than ever, he engages his opponent, and hits him with a solid left and right hook. His adversary is shocked; it's like he's fighting a new man. I'm sure you've seen the movie and or at least you know how the fight ends, so I'll leave off here.

I don't know about you, but when I watch movies like Rocky, it makes me want to leap out of my seat and shout. After a movie like that, I feel like I could sprint around the block ten times and do backflips. The truth is, we all need inspiration sometimes—an incentive to keep going. There are moments when we think, "I can't go any further." And that's when we need our "coaches" to step in and disagree with us. We need "Mickey" in our corner.

There are three coaches I can think of in my life who have inspired me to keep fighting: my spiritual coach, my business coach, and the "Head Coach," aka God. I'll tell you about them, so you can identify the people in your life and in your corner who can give you the words you need to bounce back up and go another round.

SPIRITUAL COACH

My spiritual training took a quantum leap around the time I got married and I started attending a church called Church Without Limits in my hometown. Pastor Brendan Witton married my wife and me, and he was a great source of wisdom to us for our marriage and our business. His father, Shawn Witton, led a series of weekly Bible studies, which I committed myself to after I noticed he wouldn't stop calling to invite us.

I thought, Man, this guy just won't leave us alone. Maybe he really cares? Some weeks I would make it to the class, and then I'd flake out, missing a week here and there. I'll never forget how he said, "Chris, it doesn't matter if you've made mistakes. Just keep showing up and putting yourself in front of the truth." That statement still stands strong in my heart today—that is, as long as I keep putting myself in front of the truth of God's words, knowing that it will eventually bear fruit in my life. Shawn has become a great friend, as well as a spiritual counselor in my life, and is there for me whenever I have to make tough decisions or just need advice.

It was through these Bible studies that I also met Tony Da Silva who is Mr. PMA (Positive Mental Attitude) himself. Fifteen minutes in this guy's presence and I go from being depressed to feeling like I could take on the world. He has become a great friend, and his family has become almost like a second family. I'm honored that his daughter Cayla critiqued this book. They both challenged me to make this book what it is and to not settle for mediocrity, and they've been terrific coaches.

BUSINESS COACH

There's a rap group from Canada by the name of Swollen Members that I looked up to when I first started out. These guys were massive, and I loved that they were sponsored by skateboard brands and had skaters in their music videos. I reached out to Kyle Kraft, the general manager of their record label, Battleaxe Records, about signing me. Over a period of two years, and after many emails, we started working together. He always wrote a few paragraphs with advice about the music industry, pointing me in the right direction. We exchanged emails every four months, and then in 2009, we started a working relationship. I didn't have anyone to manage me at the time. I didn't have a lot of money, but I knew I needed to grow. Right after the release of my album Citizens Activ, I hired Kyle to officially be my coach in the music business.

Kyle and I started having two-hour phone meetings every week to strategize about my music career, including every aspect of what I do. Sometimes during our brainstorming sessions I'll fire off emails during the call, and occasionally I'll get a response while he's still on the phone and we'll celebrate. Kyle not only helped me get a lot of grants, but also the knowledge, wisdom, and advice he brought into my life ignited my career like gasoline on a fire—he helped it explode! My career took massive jumps as soon as we started working together. It has never been easy, but having Kyle to help me focus on my priorities has made a huge difference. He's a great coach.

THE HEAD COACH

The most important coach of all for me has been God.

As Psalms 119:05 states: "Your word is a lamp to guide my feet and light for my path."

I've been spread-eagle on the floor many times, crying out to God in my darkest moments, or kneeling alongside my bed, praying. God has always been my comforter and guide in times of great stress. Out of the dozens and dozens of books I've read, I'm still amazed that whenever I open the Bible, it's the only book in which the words leap off the page and pierce my heart every time. Jesus said in John 16:7: "Nevertheless, I tell you the truth. It is to your advantage that I go away; for if I do not go away, the Helper will not come to you; but if I depart, I will send Him to you."

Jesus did send me the helper—the Holy Spirit. The Holy Spirit lives inside of me, to be a good guide in all that I do. When I accepted Jesus Christ as Lord and Savior, I allowed the creator of the universe to come into my life. He's been the champion coach standing behind me, fighting alongside me, at all times. When I'm going into what seems to be the toughest fight of my life, it's good to know that, "If God is for me, who could be against me." (Romans 8:31)

Here's a good example of how my "ultimate coach" God reached out to inspire me directly to keep fighting.

One night I was flying from Los Angeles to Dallas, finishing up a tour, when something strange happened. I was traveling alone, sitting in my seat, thinking about my life. I was questioning what I was doing because I was broke. No one was coming to the shows. I never saw my wife. About thirty minutes into the flight, I had to ask the flight attendant for some blankets because I was freezing-cold suddenly. It was summertime, and I must have looked funny, all bundled up like I was on the couch at home watching a movie by the fireplace.

But the chills didn't go away. They got worse. I started to shake uncontrollably, and the guy sitting next to me started staring. I tried to pin my legs down with my arms and hold myself together, but I couldn't stop shaking.

I grabbed my iPod and put on some soft worship music to calm myself down, and after a while I fell asleep. When I woke up, we were still in flight, and I had weird butterflies in my stomach. I started bawling my eyes out. Tears ran down my face, and I couldn't stop them. I had to put on my sunglasses to cover my face and use napkins to wipe up the snot running from my nose. I was a mess. Suddenly, the tears stopped, and a warm surge filled my entire body. It felt like electricity. A sweet peace came over my heart and mind that put me in a state of complete rest. It was then that I heard God's voice telling me, "Everything is going to be alright. Stop worrying."

A song came into my head called "You Said," especially the lyrics, "Ask and I'll give the nations to you, oh lord, that's the cry of my heart." I began singing it softly under my breath. I felt like I could connect the dots in my heart and mind to the dreams and visions God had given me. The plan for my life became clear. I didn't have to be afraid anymore: I knew what God wanted me to do, and it wasn't just about music, it was also about the message he had given me. I once heard Kenneth Copeland say, "Stop thinking about how you're going to get the money in, but focus on how you're going to get the word out!"

It was a hot summer day in Dallas, Texas, when I stepped off that plane and I was a changed man. It's not every day you hear the voice of God 10,000 feet in the air. My wife immediately saw the difference in me and knew something was up. I told her the story, and we embraced each other closely; we were both crying. This was a massive turning point in the Fight and things began to change! I started to fight back with more intensity, like Rocky. That's what a good coach does for you.

Now, every song I sing, and every drop of sweat that falls to the stage, is another punch in the face of my enemy! Every time I commit to recording another album, book another tour, or sign an autograph, I'm gaining ground—even if I can't see it. If I'm alone, getting depressed because nothing seems to be happening, I can remind myself that hundreds of fans all across the globe are purchasing my music and being inspired. I haven't always had the connections, and I definitely didn't have the talent, but I approached this fight with a positive mental attitude. I stopped asking, "Can I?" and started saying, "How can I?"

ETERNAL IMPACT

A few years ago I was sitting in my carpeted basement in my favorite chair thinking about all my exploits over the past ten years. I was sorting through the magazines, photos, ticket stubs, and, of course, the eight albums I've released. I came to the conclusion that I was content with what I'd accomplished, and if I didn't get any bigger—or if I quit music today—that was OK.

I've been blessed through music to inject inspiration into people's lives around the globe, and impact them, hopefully for eternity. I can't tell you how many hands I've seen raised at my shows from people ready to accept Jesus Christ as Savior. A lot of times I almost skipped sharing my story and blitzed into the next song because in my mind I thought the crowd wasn't "interested in Jesus"; but then I'd think better of it and be blown away by the response. I get emails from fans with stories of how one of my songs got them through a rough spot in college and it never gets old. I don't think there is anything more fulfilling than knowing that I've helped others reach their dreams.

But, in other ways, I'm not OK with what I've accomplished at all. It feels like I've only just begun. I have huge dreams in my heart that I have yet to see manifest, and I'm not OK with the status quo, or just settling. I once heard Robb Thompson, of the Robb Thompson Ministries say, "Today's success is tomorrow's mediocrity," and I agree.

I still want to have children and raise a family, record more music, and write more books. I want to improve my music constantly and be more creative. I only started singing two years ago and I have so much to learn. I've always wanted to play guitar, and for my thirty-third birthday, my wife bought me an acoustic guitar. I've tried to learn many times, but I think this time it's going to stick! I still have visions of a sea of faces singing out to God and seeing people stand for truth. If God wants me to do something greater, then I want to be ready for it.

Today, I stand here in the dream that I thought was lost nineteen years ago. I'm living in Southern California, faithfully married to my beautiful wife for more than ten years now. I still get to skateboard and travel the world, with my music impacting lives, one soul at a time. I still have problems and days where I feel discouraged, and I still have moments when I want to give up. A fighter is someone who can withstand criticism, failure, and loneliness. Someone who can go through the challenges, the fights, the victories, and the losses—and still come out the other side a champion. It's the individual who can continually get up again and again and keep moving toward his or her dream. The road to failure is wide and always open; I just refuse to go down it.

I've only just begun to tap into the potential that God has for me, as long as I just don't quit. So at the age of thirty-three, with over a decade of touring, writing, and performing music under my belt—I'm just getting started.

Chapter Seven
DREAMS VISIONS & GOALS

"The best way to predict your future is to create it."
—Abraham Lincoln

The purpose of this book is to inspire you to conquer your fears and take action. If it's helped you to dream again, then I feel I've succeeded. If my writing pulled you out of a dark place, helped you persevere, or be more disciplined, then I feel this book has done its job. Once we've removed fear and replaced it with faith, our courage and confidence will propel us on our quest for our dreams. Before I go I want to end this book with what I call dreams, visions, and goals. This is a call to action, a section for you to write in as you follow my roadmap, the path I used to see my dreams become reality.

KNOW YOUR ENEMY

First, let's talk about the enemy: fear. Fear is just like laziness; it creeps up on us, just like negative thoughts and bad habits. The key is to know your enemy so you can plan your response and take action quickly.

Whenever I start to get scared, I move faster. It flushes the fear out before it has a chance to root itself. I charge at the fear! The longer you wait to do something that scares you, the harder it gets. It's like skateboarding an intimidating set of stairs or surfing in strong, freezing-cold waves. Don't flinch; just do it.

I'm not promising fear won't try to rear it's ugly head again, but my goal is to equip you with the five keys to conquering it so you can win every time.

Let's look at the five keys one more time, because each key deals with fear in a different way: courage to step out and start, perseverance to keep going in spite of roadblocks and the fear of failing, mindset to eradicate fear and doubt and set your thoughts to winning, discipline to stay on course when our fears tell us to stop, and willpower to fearlessly believe in your purpose so you have the gusto to complete the mission.

I've gotten to a point in my life where I don't let fear rule it. Now it's your turn. I want you to put your finger down on this page to hold your place in the book, look up, and say this right now: I won't let fear rule my life anymore. I won't let fear rule my life anymore. I am free from fear!

DREAMS

"Dreaming is the art of creating something out of nothing." —Peter J. Daniels

Whenever I drive long distances, I love to look at the sunrise coming up over the horizon, listen to music, and dream of all I could do with what God has planned for my life. Sometimes I let my mind run wild, and create many scenarios and adventures of me doing great things. This is often how I come up with the concepts for my songs and creative ideas for performing; sometimes, though, it's just me dreaming about where I see myself in the next five to ten years. In many ways, dreaming is like taking a picture of what you are and comparing it to what you see yourself becoming. Some people are embarrassed to dream without limits because compared to their visions, they see themselves as so small. Start to see yourself the way God sees you, which is "more than a conqueror." Romans 8:37

As a boy I would fantasize about being the hero. In fact, my hero was Superman, and I would tear through the house wearing my pajamas with the red cape attached, pretending to save the world. I look back at that dream of wanting to help people, and it's what I still aspire to today. It's a good lesson on the importance of never losing that childlike innocence of dreaming.

Can I encourage you to unplug from everything, take a day or weekend off to pray? Dream and ask God to speak to you. Close your eyes and imagine yourself outside in a giant field or maybe atop a mountain with your hands raised to the sky, saying, "Here I am, Lord. Use me!" It's in these special moments I get so many ideas and God speaks to me. My wife said to me at the beginning of the year, "The key to hearing God is in the quiet places." My wife and I came to realize there are so many voices trying to get our attention, but what we need to hear is "The Voice."

TRADE IN YOUR LIFE

I invite you to take some time, and go somewhere quiet where there's no one else around. Go to the beach, or sit on a favorite park bench, or wherever inspires you, and close your eyes and just dream about what God might do with your life. Spend an hour there—or all day, if you have to.

My hero Peter J. Daniels said to me, "You can trade your life for a big dream, a small dream, or no dream, but the cost is the same.

The cost is your life!"

Can I inspire you to trade your life for a BIG dream?

"I always wanted to be a rock star. That was my childhood dream. That's what I told everybody I was going to be when I grew up." —Chester Bennington (Linkin Park)

VISIONS

"Vision is the art of seeing what is invisible to others." —Jonathan Swift

Something powerful takes place when you put your pen to paper. When you pull your dreams from the clouds and describe the vision, you breathe life into it. Sometimes fear says, "Don't write it down, someone might see it," or "What if it doesn't come to pass?" The truth is that those who write down their visions are much more likely to create them than those who don't. When you dream on paper, you can see it, touch it, and share it with others.

Vision is looking into the future and seeing what others couldn't see. Or chose not to see. Here's an example: When I start writing a song I have a vision of the finished product. I picture my fans rocking out to it live, or I imagine someone listening to the song in their bedroom and the impact it has on them with each lyric or musical note. My wife, Melanie, and I joke around that my rough demos don't sound so good. Somehow I'm able to tell if I have a hit song or not. After playing a demo for my producer, recording it, amputating some sections, and moving others around, I'll play the finished song for Melanie weeks later and many times she can't believe it's the same song I played for her before.

Having a strong vision will not only lead others, but will be a catalyst for confidence when you have doubt.

Take time right now to write out your vision in full detail, so you can see it. Describe it like a scene in a movie in which you're the main character. Write down what's around you and what you hear in the background, whether it's the ocean, the city, or birds in the trees. Even note the smells in the air. What is the weather like? How old are you? What style of clothes are you wearing in your vision?

I know it sounds silly, but when you put the effort into the details, your vision will become more alive in your spirit. This makes it more real, and fear will have to take a backseat as you claim your destiny.

"Where there is no vision the people perish."
—Proverbs 29:18

GOALS

"Goals are dreams with deadlines." —Diana Scharf

The other day I helped a friend set some goals for recording his next album. I suggested he have ten songs done by the end of the year. I know that's a lot, but I also know that if he chips away at it, he can get very close to that goal—even finishing seven songs would be a big success. The point isn't to beat yourself up if you don't make the exact goal; the point is to take action. If he doesn't shoot for ten songs, he might only have two or three songs completed by the end of the year, which is a long way from a full album. That's what setting a goal does: it puts some positive pressure on you to take action.

TAKE ACTION

"Inspiration unused is merely entertainment."
—David Bach

There has never been a better time for you to set goals and achieve your dreams. However, let me warn you, people aren't going to like it when you start getting serious about your dreams. They might think you're getting a bit of an ego, that you're being radical, or taking yourself too seriously. Your friends may criticize your dreams and goals, and your family might not understand, but remember that every critic loves to judge that which he wishes he had the nerve to do himself.

I've left some space at the end of this chapter for you to write down your dreams, visions, and goals. Remember goals need to be specific, measureable, and with a deadline for their completion. You can set short-term goals or a long-term plan for your entire life. I dare you to do it.

When you're done writing down your dreams, visions, and goals, go to imafighter.net and contact me directly or post your goals in the forum so you can join other fighters out there chasing their dreams. I believe in you; that's why I wrote this book. And I can't wait to hear what happens.

Never forget that God has a plan for your life to give you hope and a future. He didn't bring you this far just so you could stop now. So, keep fighting!

DREAM:

VISION:

GOAL:

DEADLINE:

ACKNOWLEDGEMENTS

I'd like to first thank my wife Melanie for all her hard work in designing this book—you made this into an inspirational piece of art! Also I'd like to thank you for being by my side during this crazy process and keeping me focused and balanced as we took on this massive project. I'd like to acknowledge my mother who is the strongest women I know, for giving me life, and for praying over me and dragging me to church so I could hear the truth. I'd also like to thank my sister Virginia for her continued love and support.

I'd like to thank Shannon Constantine Logan, my co-author, for responding to my unsolicited email, meeting me for tea and listening to my pitch for this book. She's done a great job taking my thoughts, stories, and ideas, and organizing them in a way that reaches so many more people. And a special thank you to our editor Carissa Bluestone, for editing the book thoroughly and giving its authors a much needed outside perspective.

I'd also like to thank Tony and Cayla Da Silva for helping me shape my ideas and not allowing me to settle on my first draft of the manuscript. You have both taught me patience and, wow, can you imagine if that first draft had gone to print? Thank you to Kyle Kraft, a great friend who has given me valuable career guidance and insights on the music industry over the years. Shawn Witton for his wisdom and positive critiques that challenged me to make this book great. To all my bandmates that gave me their input on the book while traveling. Tim Gerst for helping me launch the imafighter.net website, so it can be a beacon of inspiration for others. I'd also like to thank the Pledge Music team, Matt Lydon, Benji Rogers, Brittany Cooper, World Vision, Matthew Grieve, Doug Weber, DJ Versatile, DJ Drue, Andrew Hambleton, Dan Brio, Dave and Shannon Mischuck, our amazing printer at Tobu Print Group Marcia Mosko,

Gabe Willis at STRGT, Tim Wilson, Ian Hough, Geoff and Gary at Frontside, D.O., Kathy Hahn, Patrick Wierenga, Martin Smith, Don Pape, Gary Jay, Self Publishing, Guy Kawasaki, Air 1 Radio, Shawn Welch, Chris Stacey, Adam Messinger, Josh MacIntosh, Doug Ross, Bodan Mulholland, Ariel Hyatt, Matt Sterlecki, Carolyn Madison, Charles Van Dyke, Yozo, Shingo, Tamiko, Pastor Jonathan and Dianne Wilson, Kyle L. Olund, Geoff Bagg, Trevor McNevan, Jason Fowler, Brian Head Welch, Ryan Reis, Tooth & Nail, Tyson Paoletti, Casey Boyle, Taylor Straton, Brandon Ebel, Steve Augustine, Joel Bruyere, Jeff Goring, Kevin Richardson, Traci Scarce, Josh Ohaire, Seth Mosley, Sean Rees, Travis Blackmore, Chris Watt, Mike Crofts, Tony Patoto, Lori Mahon, Kazzer, KJ-52, Brandy Wahlman, Luke Caldwell, Mark Classen, Sam Dumcum, and Julian Rodriguez.

I'd also especially like to thank Seth Godin, Derek Sivers, Brian Tracy, John Maxwell, Dave Ramsey, Peter Daniels, Michael Hyatt, Brandon Burchard, Robert Kiyosaki, Norman Vincent Peale, Ryan Blair, and many more for writing books or creating courses that I could learn from and educate myself.

God truly is father to the fatherless and put the following men in my life as role models, who I'd like to thank: Bruce, Uncle Dave, Rudi Cardoza, Rick Reyna, Gerry Thomas, Tony Da Silva, Shawn Witton, Pastor Brendan Witton, Pastor Dwayne Hutchings, Pastor Rob Owens, Pat (Big Brother), Pastor Charlton Scullard, Josh Willis, Pastor Josh Barclay, Pastor Adam Souders, Pastor Mark Barclay, Peter Daniels, Graham Daniels, Jeremy Pearsons, Kenneth Copeland, Rob (Big Brother), Trevor McNevan, Chris Watt, Nathan Sudds, Mark Quail, and Claude Rochefort (Big Brother).

I'd also like to thank every person that has had a positive impact on my life over the past 34 years. All the speakers that despite how tired or stressed they were, stood on a platform and shared from their heart to inspire me. Every artist that dared to write a song, paint a picture, or share their creative expression. Every author that poured their blood sweat and tears into the pages of the books I've read that have shaped and transformed my life. All my fans that supported and journeyed with me over the years with my music and now my book. I'd like to thank every family that opened their home to my wife, band and I when we had nowhere to sleep. Every pastor who reached out and called me just to say a few words of encouragement. Every fan that saw me for the first time and bought my CD at a show. Every promoter who took a chance and booked me at their venue even though they had never heard of me before.

Most of all, I would like to acknowledge my Lord Jesus Christ, who by example taught me to take a stand and fight and was not a quitter. This book is for you!

SPECIAL ACKNOWLEDGMENTS

I wanted to especially thank all the Pledge Music Campaign supporters for taking a chance on a first time author before the book was released. You guys are awesome!

Josh M. Barclay, David W McSporran, Josh and Randy Willis, Adam Souders, Janina Grigat, Timothy Foley, Johannes Funk, Tracy Batchelor, Gerard Hazuka, Parker Willis, Josh Post, Linda Fox, Matthew Cook, Sean Geerholt, Douglas Marr, Rachel Ledbetter, Jeffrey Alan Parsons, Zachary Kinney, Daniel Knight, Andrea Wharff, Nicole and Christopher Jones, Nicholas Carbone, Joel Rojas, Teresa Williams, Jennifer Phillips, Larry Buxton, Adrian Kovacs, Luke McGowan, Dorothy Smith, Andrew Rivera,Vince Jones, J.T, Randy, Monica and Robin Murray, and Jillian Da Preacha Sachtleben.

CONTACT MANAFEST

For more info on Fighter go to:
WWW.IMAFIGHTER.NET

Manafest speaks frequently on the topic of conquering fear & reaching your dreams as well as the five keys. He can deliver a keynote, half-day or full day version of this content depending on your needs. If you are interested in finding out more, please visit his website at: www.imafighter.net

You can also connect with Manafest here:
FACEBOOK.COM/MANAFEST
TWITTER.COM/MANAFEST
WWW.MANAFEST.NET

MISLED YOUTH EP, 2001

MY OWN THING, 2003

CITIZENS ACTIV, 2008

CITIZENS ACTIV INSTRUMENTALS, 2009

THE CHASE INSTRUMENTALS, 2011

LIVE IN CONCERT, 2011

EPIPHANY, 2005

GLORY, 2006

GLORY INSTRUMENTALS, 2010

THE CHASE, 2011

FIGHTER, 2012

FIGHTER INSTRUMENTALS, 2012

All Manafest music available on itunes.   151

ABOUT THE AUTHOR

Christopher Scott Greenwood A.K.A. Manafest was born July 19th 1979 in Toronto, Ontario Canada. Despite an early crisis at the age of 5 losing his dad to suicide and being raised by his mother, he has picked himself off the floor countless times creating his own ladder to success. Manafest is a 3-time Juno nominated Rock artist and has toured over 13 different countries, sold over 200,000 records worldwide with songs reaching the top 10 billboard charts. His songs have been heard in major sport Networks, TV shows, Video games and been the anthem for thousands of youth across the nation. He owns and operates his own label; Manafest Productions Inc. with his wife Melanie, handling all the marketing, promotions as well as international deals with many different corporations around the globe. Chris is outspoken about his faith in Jesus Christ, a faithful husband to his wife for over 10 years and believes that anyone can change their life by changing their attitude.

COURAGE/PE
FIGHTERS MIN
LINE/WILL POV
/PERSEVERAN
MIND SET/DIS
POWER/COURA
ANCE/FIGHTE
/DISCIPLINE/
COURAGE/PE
FIGHTERS MIN